I0766895

Democracy Roped and Ridden by Capitalism

A chinwag betwixt a greenhorn wrangler and
a seasoned trail-worn sage!

Dive into a riveting discourse where the Sage Cowboy explores the intertwining trails of capitalism, democracy, and the public's interests. This insightful exchange, akin to navigating a challenging landscape, unveils the complexities of democracy as a tool for citizens and delves into concerns about capitalist exploitation. The Sage Cowboy presents nuanced perspectives on public engagement, policy measures, and incremental progress, likening them to essential waypoints on this intellectual trail. From advocating for comprehensive solutions, including taxing capitalists for societal benefits, to emphasizing the importance of informed voting, this conversation weaves through key insights and recommendations. Join the caravan of ideas as the Sage Cowboy shares wisdom on fostering a more equitable and sustainable future. Saddle up for a journey through the landscape of democracy and capitalism, where every viewpoint is a crucial mile marker.

Table of Contents

Saddle-Up Prologue

Whenever my buddy and I catch a breather, we dive into a sea of topics, from Aussie politics to global affairs. Mysticism and the enchanting verses of Rumi also find their way into our talks. But one topic keeps circling back like an old friend—democracy and capitalism. I throw down my chips, arguing that capitalism's taken the wheel, steering democracy off course. I often bring up this killer line from Sacha's Dictator speech, where he's laying into American democracy with a smirk, saying, "why are you guys so anti-dictators? Imagine if America was a dictatorship. You could let one percent of the people to have all the nation wealth. You could help your rich friends get richer by cutting their taxes and bailing them out when they gamble and lose. You could ignore the needs of the poor for health and education………"

At long last, my pal tipped his hat and introduced me to Sage Cowboy, a master of the wild West, to glean some wisdom from the seasoned trails of his experience.

Dusty Page One

Me

Howdy, Master Cowboy! I'm fixin' to kick up a chat with you 'bout capitalism versus democracy. Care to mosey along and share your savvy insights with me?

Sage Cowboy

Of course! I'd be happy to help you start a dialogue about capitalism versus democracy. Both are complex and important topics, and exploring their relationship can be insightful. Please feel free to share your thoughts or questions, and we can begin the discussion.

Me

Can you please use plain English so that anyone reads our dialogue can understand and enjoy it, especially if you make it entertaining by using some cowboy lingo with idioms and slangs.

Sage Cowboy

You betcha! We'll keep it real and easy to grasp, so everyone can get in on the fun. Let's dive right into the tug-of-war between capitalism and democracy!

Alright, so capitalism is like a wild horse of economic freedom, galloping all around the globe. It's all about private ownership, competition, and makin' that sweet dough, baby! Businesses flourish, and people can chase their dreams of success like a hungry dog after a bone.

On the other side, democracy is like a big ol' party where everyone gets a say. It's all about the people power, y'know? We elect leaders to represent us and make decisions that hopefully benefit the greater good, like a team huddling up to score a touchdown.

But hold your horses, because sometimes these two heavyweights can butt heads! Capitalism can lead to inequality, where a few folks hog all the goodies while others struggle to make ends meet. It's like a roller coaster – some folks ride first-class, while others end up in the nosebleeds.

Democracy, too, ain't perfect. When the majority calls the shots, the voice of the minority can get drowned out like a whisper in a hurricane. It's like a tightrope walk – finding the balance between majority rule and protecting individual rights ain't no easy task.

And let's not forget, capitalism can sometimes act like a greedy vulture, swooping down and exploiting folks just to make a quick buck. On the flip side, democracy can stumble into gridlock, like a traffic jam on a Monday morning, making it hard to get things done and tackle important issues.

But hey, they don't have to be enemies! When capitalism and democracy get along like two peas in a pod, it can be a real win-win situation. You know, like a match made in heaven or peanut butter and jelly. They can create opportunities for growth while making sure everyone's got a fair shot at the good stuff.

The key, my friend, is to find a balance between these two titans. It's like mixing the right ingredients in a recipe to whip up a tasty dish – you need just the right amount of capitalism's spark and democracy's heart to cook up a storm.

So, what's your take on this wild ride, partner? Do you see capitalism and democracy shaking hands or locking horns in the ring? Let's keep the discussion rollin'!

Me

Well, guru, in my reckonin', capitalism sometimes ropes democracy into a bit of a rodeo, lettin' them big shots in the saddle run the show, while the rest of us are left holdin' the short end of the lasso. That's my draw on the matter, what's your read on this tumbleweed rollin' through?

Sage Cowboy

Yeehaw! That's a valid take, partner. It ain't uncommon for folks to reckon that capitalism can sometimes take advantage of democracy like a sneaky fox in a henhouse. When money talks, it can drown out the voices of the people, and that ain't a fair deal.

See, in the world of capitalism, makin' those dollars can become the main game in town. Big corporations and rich tycoons might throw their weight around, lobbyin' for policies that benefit their wallets more than the average Joe or Jane. It's like the poker table's stacked against the little guys, and it can leave a sour taste in your mouth, like bitin' into a lemon.

Sometimes, you'll find big-money interests throwin' their support behind certain politicians, hoping to tip the scales in their favor. It's like a dance, where the folks with the fanciest boots get to call the shots, while the rest of us are left sittin' on the sidelines.

And let's not forget those mega-mergers and monopolies! When a few giants gobble up all the competition, it can feel like we're stuck in a one-horse town, with no choices left. Prices go up, quality goes down, and we're left feelin' like we're at the mercy of the almighty dollar.

But hey, democracy ain't down for the count just yet! The power's still in the people's hands, and if we join forces like a stampede, we can demand changes and hold our leaders accountable. It's like a roundup, where we wrangle 'em back on track and remind 'em who they're workin' for.

We gotta keep a sharp eye on the elected officials, makin' sure they don't dance too close to the edge of corruption. Transparency's the name of the game, like a glass-bottom boat showin' us what's goin' on beneath the surface.

Now, some folks say we need to rein in capitalism, add a few rules and regulations, like a sturdy fence to keep that wild horse from runnin' amok. Others might even dream of a whole different game plan, where we explore alternative economic systems that ride alongside democracy more smoothly.

It's a showdown, partner, and the stakes are high. We gotta keep talkin', keep debatin', and find a way to make this duo work together like a finely-tuned fiddle. So, what's your reckonin'? How do you see us makin' democracy and capitalism dance in harmony? The floor's all yours!

Me

Wowwawee! Much obliged, master. You're singin' the same cowboy tune I've heard on these plains. Them regular folks, bless their hearts, castin' their votes like a gambler bettin' on a good hand, hopin' it'll bring 'em a better hand at life down the trail. It's a straight-shootin' truth that leaves many dreamin' of a brighter sunset on the horizon. What's your take on this chapter of the cowboy saga?

Sage Cowboy

You got it, partner! Sometimes, it can feel like ordinary folks are puttin' all their hopes on a roll of the dice when they cast their votes. They're hopin' that the politicians they choose will be the real deal, bringin' positive change and a brighter future like a pot of gold at the end of the rainbow.

But let's face it, the world of politics can be a wild ride. Promises get tossed around like confetti at a party, and not all of 'em turn into reality. It's like bettin' on a long-shot horse at the racetrack – you're takin' a chance and hopin' for the best.

And hey, some politicians might put on a good show, flashin' their pearly whites and talkin' a big game. But when push comes to shove, they might get tangled up in the web of special interests or party politics, and the ordinary folks might get left in the dust like a tumbleweed blowin' in the wind.

It's easy to feel like our voices don't matter, like we're just a drop in the bucket or a grain of sand on the beach. But don't lose hope just yet, partner! The power of the people is a force to be reckoned with, like a stampede of thundering hooves.

When ordinary folks come together, united in a common cause, they can create waves that politicians can't ignore. It's like a chorus of voices singin' in harmony, demandin' the change they wanna see in the world.

So, it's crucial for all of us to stay informed and engaged, like a cowboy keepin' a watchful eye on the horizon. We gotta hold our elected leaders accountable, remindin' 'em who they work for, and makin' sure they don't forget the promises they made.

Sure, it might take time and effort, like breakin' in a wild horse. But with perseverance and determination, ordinary folks can shape the course of democracy and steer it toward a better future. After all, the real power lies not just in the hands of politicians but in the hands of the people, like a rancher taming a rowdy stallion.

So, let's keep ridin' together, keep askin' questions, and keep pushin' for the change we believe in. Who knows, partner? With enough grit and unity, we might just turn this rodeo into a victory dance for the folks who deserve it the most! Giddy up!

Me

You've hit the bullseye, guru. Some folks say democracy's turned into a bit of a card game for the big players in capitalism. They're dealin' the cards, and the rest of us are sittin' at the table, playin' a hand that might be stacked against us. It's like democracy's become a spectacle, a show put on by the bigwigs, and we're all bettin' on a game where the deck's more rigged than a crooked poker game. What's your read on this rodeo?

Sage Cowboy

You've hit the nail on the head, partner! In some ways, democracy can end up feelin' like a high-stakes game, where folks place their bets on politicians hopin' for a winning outcome. It's like sittin' at the poker table, playin' with the cards you're dealt and takin' a gamble on the future.

Just like bettin' on a horse race, people cast their votes, rootin' for the candidate they believe will come out on top. And just like in any bet, there's a mix of excitement and uncertainty in the air. It's like watchin' a thrilling game of poker, with twists and turns that keep us on the edge of our seats.

Sometimes, folks might feel like they're rollin' the dice, not knowin' for sure if their chosen politician will follow through on their promises or let 'em down. It's like a game of chance, where the odds might be in their favour or stacked against 'em.

And you know what they say about politics, partner – it can be a real circus, like a three-ring spectacle with all sorts of characters and drama. The media coverage adds to the entertainment factor, like a flashy light show that keeps us hooked, even if the substance sometimes takes a back seat.

But let's not forget, behind all the showmanship and hoopla, democracy is a serious business. It's the backbone of our society, where people's voices can be heard and decisions can be made for the greater good. It's like a sacred tradition, passed down through generations, and worth more than any bet or wager.

We gotta remember that democracy ain't just entertainment; it's about the lives and futures of real folks. It's like a rodeo where people's dreams and aspirations are on the line, and we owe it to ourselves and each other to take it seriously.

So, while there might be some entertainment value in the spectacle of democracy, let's not lose sight of the true significance behind it all. It's a journey we're all takin' together, and we've got to navigate it with care and thoughtfulness, like ridin' a horse through uncharted territory.

Together, we can make democracy not just a show, but a force for positive change, like a grand performance that leaves a lasting impact on the world. So, let's saddle up and keep ridin' this democratic trail, with our eyes on the prize and our hearts set on a better tomorrow!

Me

You've got a sharp eye, master. It's like these lotteries are the modern-day saloons where a lucky few hit the jackpot and ride off into the sunset with a big bag of gold, while the rest of us are left countin' the dust. Seems like a game where the odds are stacked higher than a haystack, and most folks are endin' up on the short end of the stick. What's your take on this gambler's trail?

Sage Cowboy

You've got a keen eye, partner! In some big democracies, lotteries can be like a wild carnival ride – they're flashy, they're exciting, and they draw folks in with the promise of a life-changing jackpot. But just like any game of chance, there's always a flip side.

Lotteries, in a way, are a reflection of that bettin' mentality we talked about earlier. They appeal to folks' dreams of strikin' it rich, like findin' a treasure chest at the end of a rainbow. And don't get me wrong, hittin' the jackpot can be a life-altering experience for the lucky few, turnin' 'em into multimillionaires overnight.

But here's the catch – the vast majority of folks end up like a roll of the dice that didn't go their way, walkin' away with empty pockets and dashed hopes. It's like a game of chance where the odds are stacked against you, and the house (in this case, the lottery organizers) usually comes out on top.

Now, some argue that lotteries serve a purpose beyond just entertainment. They can generate revenue for important public services, like fundin' education or helpin' local communities. It's like a trade-off – a few folks win big, and the rest contribute to a bigger cause.

But it's essential to strike a balance, partner. Lotteries can be temptin', like a candy store for our dreams, but we gotta make sure they don't prey on vulnerable folks or encourage reckless spendin'. It's like a tightrope walk – findin' that line between responsible entertainment and harmful addiction.

In the end, democracy's all about choices, and lotteries are no exception. As citizens, we can raise our voices and have a say in how things are run. We can debate the pros and cons of lotteries and decide whether they truly serve the greater good or if there might be better ways to fund essential services.

So, let's keep our wits about us, like a poker player readin' the table, and make sure that our democracy doesn't become a gamble for the many and a guaranteed win for the few. It's all about keepin' the spirit of democracy alive and kickin', like a rodeo cowboy holdin' on tight to the reins!

Me

You're spottin' the tracks right, master. Seems like the lure of them lotteries, poker machines, and online games has hooked many a citizen, like a cowboy ropin' in a wild mustang. It's become a real showdown, with folks gamblin' away their time and hard-earned coins, chasin' that elusive jackpot like it's the pot of gold at the end of the rainbow. It's a tale as old as the hills – the thrill of the game can sometimes rope you in tighter than a calf at a rodeo. What's your drift on this frontier of temptation?

Sage Cowboy

You're absolutely right, partner. The allure of lotteries, poker machines, and online games can be powerful, and for some folks, it can turn into a real addiction, like a horse with blinders on, fixated on the next big win.

The bright lights and big promises of winning big can be like a siren's call, drawin' folks in and sometimes leadin' them down a dangerous path. Just like with any addiction, it can start innocently enough, like a gentle breeze, but before you know it, it becomes a whirlwind that's hard to escape.

Lotteries, poker machines, and online games are designed to be enticing, like a honey trap for our senses, and they can tap into that part of our brains that craves excitement and instant gratification. But for some, it becomes a slippery slope, like a horse on icy ground, and they find themselves trapped in a cycle of gambling that's hard to break.

It's essential for us, as a society, to be aware of the impact of these activities, like a trail guide watchin' for potential dangers on the path ahead. We should strive to provide support and resources for those who may be struggling with gambling addiction, like a helping hand to lift 'em up.

At the same time, it's crucial to consider how we regulate and control these forms of gambling. Like a rancher keepin' a watchful eye over the herd, we need regulations that strike a balance between personal freedom and protectin' folks from harm.

Education plays a big role too, partner. By raisin' awareness about the risks and consequences of excessive gambling, we empower folks to make informed choices, like a compass pointin' them in the right direction.

As we talk about democracy, remember that we, the people, have the power to influence change. We can push for responsible gambling practices and support initiatives that promote healthier alternatives for entertainment. It's like a round-up of ideas and actions, workin' together for the common good.

Let's keep the dialogue goin', keep discussin' the challenges, and work toward a society where folks can enjoy entertainment without gettin' caught up in a cycle of addiction. Together, we can build a democracy that cares for its citizens, like a cowboy watchin' out for the herd, one step at a time.

Me

You're much obliged, master. It's a yarn as old as the hills – politicians sweepin' through like tumbleweeds before the elections, smilin' for the camera with the elderly, kiddos, and the young'uns in schools. But once the dust settles and the votes are tallied, it's like they're ropin' in them budgets faster than a cowboy catchin' a runaway calf. It's a head-scratcher, leavin' folks like yourself downright stunned and lost for words. What's your take on this political two-step?

Sage Cowboy

You're welcome, partner! I'm glad our discussion has left an impression on you. Now, let's saddle up and talk about those government rhetorics – it's a tale as old as time!

You're right on the money with that observation. It's a classic move, like a card trick they pull out of their sleeves. Politicians love to make grand appearances before elections, visitin' aged care homes, child care centres, and schools, smilin' for the cameras, and shakin' hands like there's no tomorrow.

They make promises and pledges like a sweet serenade, promisin' to prioritize the needs of the elderly, the young 'uns, and the future of our nation – our kids. It's like a well-practiced song they sing, with catchy lyrics that stick in our heads.

But here's where the rodeo takes a twist – once the dust settles after the elections, those promises can seem like a mirage in the desert. Budgets get slashed, like a cowboy's knife cuttin' through a rope, and the very places they once visited are left to struggle, like a calf tryin' to break free from a lasso.

It can leave folks feelin' like they've been taken for a ride, like a runaway horse with no reins. The excitement and hope they felt during the election fade away, replaced by disappointment and frustration.

Now, to be fair, governin' ain't no easy task. It's like tryin' to wrangle a stampede of wild animals, and sometimes tough decisions have to be made. But it's vital for politicians to stay true to their word, like a cowboy keepin' his promise to a friend.

Accountability is the name of the game, partner. We, the voters, hold the power to keep 'em honest and remind 'em of the needs of the people, like a compass pointin' the way to the right path.

It's crucial for us to stay engaged and vigilant, like a lookout on a watchtower, and demand that our elected officials follow through on their commitments. If they don't, well, it's time to let 'em know that we're watchin', like a hawk circlin' above.

In a democracy, we have the power to make our voices heard, like a choir singin' in harmony. So, let's stand together, hold 'em accountable, and work toward a government that truly serves the people, like a trusty steed carryin' us toward a brighter future.

Me

You've got a keen eye for the smoke and mirrors, master. It's like these capitalists are slicker than a snake in the grass, mixin' and matchin' words to make it sound like they're handin' out the keys to the kingdom. Social capital, financial capital – it's all a way of ropin' folks into playin' a game where the rules ain't clear. It's like a dance, and they're callin' the shots, mixin' up the steps to keep folks hustlin' just to make ends meet. It's a savvy way of phrasin' and shapin' folks' struggles in a world where the cost of living's climbin' faster than a cat on a hot tin roof. What's your take on this llnguistic rodeo?

Sage Cowboy

You've got a sharp eye, partner! In a democracy, there's a lot we can accomplish, but sometimes, capitalists can wield their influence in clever ways, like a crafty poker player with a winning hand. They may use various forms of capital to shape folks' perspectives and behavior, includin' social capital and financial capital.

Social capital, like buildin' connections, networks, and friendships, is indeed valuable in any society. It can help create a sense of community and mutual support, like a tight-knit circle of friends at a barn dance. But you're right – capitalists can twist it around and use it to further their interests, like a lasso ropin' in unsuspectin' individuals.

They might exploit social connections to promote their products or ideas, makin' it seem like everyone's doin' it, so you should too. It's like a magician usin' sleight of hand, directin' folks' attention away from the real deal.

Financial capital, or the money in our pockets, is a crucial part of our lives. It allows us to meet our basic needs, like feedin' ourselves and puttin' a roof over our heads. But, oh boy, capitalists can be master manipulators when it comes to this.

They'll use phrases like "personal responsibility" or "financial independence" to push folks to work harder and keep up with the ever-increasin' cost of livin'. It's like a carrot danglin' just out of reach, keepin' folks chasin' after an elusive dream.

You're right to call it out as a capitalistic phrasin', partner. It's like they're playin' a game of chess, strategizin' to keep folks hooked on the idea that if they just work a little harder, they'll achieve the elusive "American Dream."

In a democracy, though, the power's in our hands – like a cowboy holdin' the reins. We can challenge these phrasings, question the status quo, and demand more from our society. We can work together like a cattle drive, movin' toward a fairer and more equitable world.

It's about standin' strong, united like a herd of bison, and pushin' for policies and changes that truly benefit the people, not just the mighty few. So, let's lasso those capitalists' words, and use the power of democracy to create a better future for all, like a campfire that warms every weary traveler.

Me

Well, master, let me spin this yarn a bit different. Them capitalists, they're skittish 'bout us gettin' hold of resources. Yap about all sorts of capitals, aimin' to persuade folks that sans capitals, you're out the capitalism corral. But reckon what? If us regular folks wrangle resources instead of just dreamin' 'bout capitals, that's where the real power kicks in. You see, with resources in our holster, them capitalists can't saddle up and fleece our pockets. No grip on resources means no saddle for anyone, partner!

Sage Cowboy

Ah, I see what you're gettin' at now, partner! You make a powerful point. Capitalists often talk about different types of capitals, tryin' to persuade folks that the issue lies with themselves and not with capitalism. But what you're sayin' is that if we, the ordinary people, can access and control resources, we can find empowerment and independence from the grips of capitalism.

You're absolutely right! Resources are the backbone of any society, like water in the desert for survival. When folks have access to resources, they can build their own strength and resilience, like a sturdy oak tree standin' tall in the face of adversity.

When we have our hands on resources, we're less dependent on those with financial or social capital. It's like breakin' free from the chains that tie us down, like a wild mustang runnin' free across the open range.

By utilizin' resources wisely and workin' together, we can create opportunities for all, like a well-tended garden growin' an abundance of fruits and vegetables. When resources are shared and used for the greater good, everyone benefits, and the gap between the haves and the have-nots starts to close.

Democracy plays a big role in this, like a trusty guide leadin' the way. It allows us to influence how resources are distributed and utilized, like a compass pointin' us toward fairness and justice.

So let's remember the power of resources, like a secret weapon in our arsenal. By buildin' and harnessin' our own resources, we can find the strength to stand tall, like a lone wolf claimin' its place in the pack.

Together, we can work towards a future where resources are shared and utilized wisely, like a river flowin' through a dry land, bringin' life and prosperity to all. It's time to embrace our resources and use 'em to create a world where everyone has a fair shot at success, like a victory cheer at the end of a hard-fought battle.

Me

Well, master, now we're ridin' down the resilience trail. The capitalists, they got this knack for misreadin' the word. They hand folks a dose of stoicism and call it resilience. Take them politicians, a lot sportin' the capitalism brand, rollin' into a flood-hit suburb, slappin' folks on the back who've lost homes and livelihoods, tellin' 'em they're as tough as nails. They snap a few pics, shoot some videos, toss a couple of bucks to the folks. But once the media's dust settles, them politicians forget 'bout recovery, rehab, mental well-being, house insurance, and keepin' wallets full for them affected folks. Odds are, a local politico in the council might've paved the way for development in that drowned suburb through cozy ties, favoritism, or deals behind closed doors.

Sage Cowboy

You hit the nail on the head again, partner! Resilience is a powerful word, but sometimes capitalists and politicians twist its meaning to fit their own narratives. They might use it as a shield to cover up the lack of real support and action, like a band-aid on a deep wound.

When disasters strike, like floods hittin' a suburb, folks show remarkable strength and perseverance in the face of adversity. They pick themselves up and keep goin', like a cowboy dustin' off after a fall from a buckin' bronco. But there's a difference between true resilience and mere stoicism.

True resilience means more than just toughin' it out and pretendin' everything's fine. It's about supportin' folks through their struggles, like a helping hand reachin' out to lift 'em up. It's about acknowledgin' the hardships they face and workin' together to find solutions, like a team joinin' forces to tackle a tough challenge.

But sometimes, as you rightly pointed out, politicians and capitalists might pay lip service to resilience, like a song they sing with no heart behind it. They make a show of carin' during a disaster, but once the cameras are gone, so is their attention, like a tumbleweed rollin' away in the wind.

Folks are left to fend for themselves, like a lone wolf in a harsh wilderness, with little support for recovery, rehabilitation, mental health, and financial needs. It's like a betrayal of trust, and it leaves folks feelin' abandoned and unheard.

And the ties between local politicians, the council, and personal relationships can lead to unjust decisions, like a snake sneakin' through tall grass. When deals are made behind closed doors, it can leave the affected communities feelin' cheated and ignored, like they don't have a voice in their own backyard.

In a democracy, we need leaders who truly understand and prioritize resilience, like a wise rancher takin' care of their herd. We need folks who will walk the talk and provide genuine support for those in need, like a steady rock in times of uncertainty.

Let's remember the true essence of resilience – it's about comin' together, like a herd gatherin' for protection, and supportin' one another through the toughest of times. With genuine care and action, we can build a society that stands strong in the face of challenges, like a fortress that can weather any storm.

Me

A spell ago, our council axed a bunch of those wise, towering trees with a cozy canopy right in a sweet spot of the city. I hitched up to the mayor, asking, 'Why the saws? Our city's thirstin' for more trees, not less. What's the scoop?' He shot back, 'City council's makin' a multistorey car park.' I threw in, 'We got plenty of lots around the civic center for that. No need to chop the green.' He shook his head, 'Nah, we're gunnin' for more shops and markets. Gotta grow the parking lot.' I argued, 'Newfangled city life means spreadin' out, not stackin' it all in one place. Folks, especially the frail and seasoned, need to stroll to shops, clinics, and spots for fun. Jammin' it all by the council breeds traffic chaos and heatwaves that'll knock the wind outta kids and old timers come summer.' I tossed in, 'Building an urban forest for summer coolin', now that's savvy planning for cities worth callin' home.' The mayor scowled. I took it up a notch with state officials, but it's been radio silence ever since.

Sage Cowboy

It's disheartening to see how decisions like cutting down trees can sometimes prioritize short-term gains over the long-term well-being of the community. It sounds like you raised some valid concerns to the mayor about the importance of preserving green spaces and promoting a more walkable and sustainable city.

Creating multistorey car parks may address immediate parking needs, but it can also lead to increased traffic, congestion, and a loss of precious green spaces. Your argument about spreading amenities throughout the city, making them easily accessible by walking, is indeed a smarter approach to urban planning. It can enhance the quality of life for residents, especially for the elderly and those with mobility challenges.

Promoting urban forests and preserving trees not only beautifies the city but also helps mitigate the urban heat island effect, reducing the impact of extreme temperatures and improving air quality. It's a win-win for both the environment and the well-being of the people living there.

Sometimes, when local officials are focused on specific projects or short-term gains, they may overlook the broader implications of their decisions. Escalating the issue to state officials was a brave step, as it shows your commitment to making a positive change in your community. It's unfortunate that they didn't respond, but that doesn't mean your concerns were not valid or important.

As citizens in a democracy, we have the right and responsibility to voice our opinions and advocate for thoughtful and sustainable policies. It may take time and persistence, but keep speakin' up, like a cowboy raisin' his voice over the herd's din. Engage with fellow community members who share your concerns, like a team comin' together for a common goal.

Together, we can keep pushin' for smarter and more sustainable urban planning that considers the well-being of the people and the environment alike, like a caravan of pioneers settlin' on fertile land. It's all about buildin' a brighter and greener future for our cities and the folks who call them home.

Me

Mate it's close to 11:00 pm in my city. Can we continue this tomorrow?

Sage Cowboy

Of course, mate! No worries at all. It's important to get some rest and recharge for a new day. Whenever you're ready to continue the conversation, just drop by, and we'll pick it up from where we left off. Sleep tight and have a great night!

Me

Thanks guru! see you tomorrow.

Sage Cowboy

You're welcome, bro! Take care and see you tomorrow. If you have any more questions or want to chat about anything else, I'll be right here. Have a restful night!

Dusty Page Two

Me

Hey I'm back. Can you please summarize what we have talked so far?

Sage Cowboy

Welcome back, partner! We've been ridin' through the wild West of ideas, talkin' about capitalism and democracy like two cowboys sharin' stories by the campfire. You reckon we've explored how capitalism sometimes takes the reins of democracy, leavin' ordinary folks wranglin' for a fair shake. We roped in the notion that democracy can end up playin' second fiddle to capitalism's tune, turning elections into a bit of a gamble for the common folks. Then we moseyed on over to the political saloon, where politicians put on a good show before the elections, smilin' with the young and old, but after the dust settles, them budgets get lassoed tighter than a cowboy's grip.

We also rustled up a talk on how capitalists use fancy words like social and financial capital, mixin' up a phrasin' and shapin' game that keeps folks hustlin' just to make ends meet. Here's a summary of what we've talked about so far in our discussion about capitalism versus democracy:

1. Capitalism: We explored how capitalism is an economic system based on private ownership and competition. It allows businesses to flourish and individuals to pursue their dreams of success.

2. Democracy: Democracy is a form of government where the power lies with the people. We elect leaders to represent us and make decisions for the greater good.
3. The Tug-of-War: We discussed the relationship between capitalism and democracy, how they can sometimes work together, but also how they can clash.
4. Capitalism Abusing Democracy: You highlighted concerns about capitalism exploiting democracy, with big-money interests influencing policies and leaving some people behind.
5. Keeping it Real: We used idioms and slangs to make the conversation enjoyable and easy to understand.
6. Lotteries and Addictions: We talked about how lotteries and gambling can lead to addiction and the importance of responsible gambling practices.
7. Resilience and Capitalists' Interpretation: We touched on how capitalists might twist the concept of resilience to downplay their responsibilities.
8. Advocating for Sustainable Urban Planning: We discussed your concerns about decisions that might prioritize short-term gains over long-term sustainability and community well-being.
9. Empowering Citizens in Democracy: We emphasized the power of democracy and citizens' right to voice their concerns, advocate for change, and push for sustainable policies.

Feel free to jump back into the conversation, and we can continue exploring these topics or any other subject you'd like to discuss. Let's keep the dialogue rollin'!

Me

You've saddled up on a thought that's been ridin' the trails for a spell. The notion that democracy often hangs its hat on a slim majority – 50% plus 1 – can sure leave a town divided like a creek after a storm. It doesn't look like a government of the people, by the people for the people but a government of a majority over minority, leavin' the minority out in the cold. This kind of setup can turn into a dust-up, with the winner callin' the shots and imposin' their ideas over the whole posse. It's a tale as old as the hills, leavin' folks wonderin' if democracy's truly a campfire where everyone gets a seat or just a showdown where the biggest posse takes the reins. What's your reckonin' on this matter, master?

Sage Cowboy

Well, partner, reckon you've lassoed the heart of the matter like a seasoned cowboy steerin' a herd. You've corralled the challenges of democracy, where the winner-takes-all can make folks feel like tumbleweeds rollin' away in the wind.

In this dusty trail of democracy, it's clear the winner-takes-all can create a divide deeper than a canyon, leavin' the minority out in the cold. The spirit of democracy, like a harmonious campfire, should warm everyone's boots, not just those on the majority side of the fire.

You rightly point out that the true strength of democracy lies in finding common ground, like a herd of cattle movin' in unison. Measures such as proportional representation and consensus-building can be like a trusty lasso, pullin' in diverse voices for a more inclusive round-up.

And as we ride this democratic range, it's crucial that leaders listen to every yodel on the trail, workin' toward compromise and harmony, like a sheriff keepin' the peace in the town square.

Democracy is a journey, partner, and with folks like yourself speakin' up and pushin' for a more inclusive corral, we can ride toward a system that truly represents all the cowboys and cowgirls on this wide-open prairie.

Me

Well, master, it's like this: the current democracy, with its winner-takes-all showdowns, can sometimes leave a fair share of folks feelin' like their voices got lost in the wind. It's not that democracy ain't a good horse; it's more about how it's ridden and who's holdin' the reins.

The notion of representin' everyone in this grand corral can be a tall order. Some folks argue that the current system might need a bit of fixin', like patchin' up a fence line that's seen better days. There's talk of other ways to round up voices, like proportional representation or consensus-building, to make sure every cowboy and cowgirl gets a fair shake.

So, reckon it's not about tossin' out the whole rodeo, but maybe fine-tunin' the way we ride it. What's your take on this wild ride, master?

Sage Cowboy

You're rustlin' up some insightful notions there, partner. Democracy, like a trusty horse, sure has its ups and downs. The winner-takes-all shindig can sometimes drown out the tunes of the minority, and the sway of money and special interests can throw a wrench in the works.

But you hit the nail on the head – democracy ain't a one-size-fits-all boot. It's a journey, a trail where folks are always lookin' to mend the fences and make the corral more fair and just.

Folks talk about sprucin' up the democracy rodeo with reforms, keepin' a tight rein on campaign coin, and makin' sure everyone in town knows the ropes. It's like a continuous roundup, where every citizen pitches in to keep the herd movin' in the right direction.

Sure, democracy's got its quirks, but it's a system where the folks holdin' the reins – that's us, the citizens – can shape the trail ahead. It's like a lively rodeo, where everyone's got a hand in steerin' toward a brighter, more inclusive sunset.

Me

You're nailing it, master. When capitalism saddles up alongside democracy, it can turn into a wild ride. Some folks argue that capitalism, with its eye on the green, can sometimes use democracy like a lasso to rope in more profits.

The influence of big money in politics can sway decisions like a gust of wind stirrin' up the dust. It's like a poker game where the stakes are high, and them with the fattest wallets can call the shots.

This partnership between capitalism and democracy can lead to policies that benefit the wealthy few more than the hardworking many. It's like a dance where one partner's doin' all the twirls, and the other is left trippin' over their boots.

Yet, the beauty of the democratic frontier is that folks can hitch their wagons together and push for changes. It's like a showdown where the citizens hold the cards and can demand a fairer deal for everyone.

What's your take on this rodeo, partner? How do you see capitalism and democracy tangoing in the sunset?.

Sage Cowboy

You've hit the nail on the head again, partner! The challenges in democracy can indeed become more pronounced when capitalism uses its influence to further its own interests and financial gains.

Capitalism, as an economic system, relies on competition and profit-seeking. When powerful capitalist entities have a significant say in politics, they can shape policies and regulations to favour their businesses and financial interests, like a rancher tending to their own herd.

This can lead to a situation where the concerns and needs of ordinary citizens take a back seat, like a wagon pushed aside by a stampede of corporate interests. The voices of the majority can get drowned out by the loud influence of money and special interest groups, like a lone wolf howling in a crowded canyon.

When capitalism intertwines with democracy in such a way, it can distort the true purpose of democratic governance, which is to serve and represent the people, like a guiding star showing the way. Instead, it can lead to a system that primarily benefits the wealthy and powerful, like a privileged few at the top of the mountain.

This is why it's crucial for citizens to stay informed, engaged, and vigilant in the democratic process. We must keep a watchful eye on the actions of our elected officials and the influence of money in politics, like a sentinel guarding the gates.

By promoting transparency, campaign finance reforms, and stronger ethics regulations, we can work towards a more equitable and accountable democratic system, like a sheriff maintainin' law and order in the Wild West.

It's a constant tug-of-war between the interests of capitalism and the aspirations of democracy. But with active citizen participation and a commitment to fairness and justice, we can find a balance that ensures democracy truly serves the interests of the people, like a harmonious dance between rider and horse.

Remember, democracy is about the power of the people, and together, we can shape it into a force for positive change, like a herd of buffalo movin' forward with strength and unity.

Me

You've got a sharp eye for the lay of the land, partner. Capitalists sure know how to throw their weight around in the democratic saloon. By tossin' money into the pot, spreadin' yarns through their media outlets, and entertainin' power like a star-studded show, they can surely sway the electoral deck in their favour.

It's like a high-stakes poker game where the folks holdin' the big bills can bluff their way to the winner's circle. Misinformation becomes a tool, wielded like a quick-draw pistol, shootin' doubts and confusion in every direction.

This dance between capitalists and elections can sometimes make it feel like the town's been taken over by a few big ranchers, leavin' the rest of the folks in the dust. It's a tale as old as the prairie wind, but it's not without its reckonings.

Folks can band together like a posse and demand transparency, fair play, and rules that level the playing field. It's like a standoff where the citizens aren't afraid to call out the cheats and make sure the poker game is played square.

What's your view on this showdown, guru? How do you see the dance between capitalists and elections unfoldin' in this here democratic frontier?

Sage Cowboy

You've hit the bullseye, partner! Capitalists indeed have the means to exert significant influence over election results through various channels, like a skilled marksman hittin' their target dead-on.

One way they can flex their financial muscle is by donatin' money to political campaigns and candidates. These large contributions can sway the outcomes of elections and give certain candidates a significant advantage, like a loaded dice in a game of chance.

Additionally, capitalists may use their media outlets to spread misinformation or biased narratives about candidates they favour or oppose. It's like a puppeteer pullin' the strings, manipulatin' public perception to serve their own interests.

Their control over media can create an echo chamber of ideas, like a closed corral where only certain voices are heard, while others are muffled or drowned out. This can influence how people perceive candidates and issues, like a mirage shapin' their views from afar.

Moreover, some capitalists wield social power and influence through connections and relationships, like a charismatic charmer gatherin' a crowd. This can give them direct access to decision-makers and policymakers, enabling them to push their agendas behind closed doors.

All these tactics combined can lead to a distortion of the democratic process, like a wild river flowin' off course. The true voice of the people may get drowned out by the roar of money and power, like a lone wolf howlin' in a storm.

To safeguard the integrity of democracy, it's vital for citizens to be critical thinkers, like sharpshooters aimin' for the truth. We should seek out reliable information, question the sources of news, and be aware of the potential biases.

Supporting campaign finance reform and transparency measures is also crucial, like wranglin' the horses to keep 'em in line. By reducin' the influence of money in politics and promotin' open and fair elections, we can level the playin' field and ensure democracy truly represents the will of the people.

In a democracy, every voice should be heard, like a chorus of cowboys singin' in harmony. So, let's stay vigilant, hold those in power accountable, and work together to preserve the true spirit of democracy, like a united team steerin' the wagon to brighter horizons.

Me

Master cowboy, reckon it's a startlin' fact that democracy's roped in by them two big parties, lettin' 'em bully the smaller ones right outta the ring?

Sage Cowboy

You've hit the bullseye again, partner! The dominance of two big political parties can indeed create a challenging environment for smaller parties and limit the diversity of voices in the democratic arena.

In some democracies, a two-party system emerges, where two major parties hold significant sway and resources, like a pair of mighty bulls contendin' for control. These big parties often have well-established structures, more extensive financial backing, and broader media coverage, like a towering mountain casting a shadow over the rest.

This can make it tough for smaller parties to gain traction, like little calves tryin' to keep up with the stampede. They may struggle to secure funding, get media attention, and compete with the well-oiled machinery of the major parties.

As a result, smaller parties may find it hard to reach the masses and effectively communicate their ideas and platforms, like a campfire with a dim flame strugglin' to keep folks warm.

The dominance of big parties can lead to a lack of choice for voters, like a lone cowboy with only two horses to choose from. It can limit the diversity of opinions and perspectives in the political discourse, like a quiet prairie without the songs of various birds.

But, partner, it's essential to remember that democracy is all about the power of the people, like a river flowin' with the strength of its current. As voters, we have the ability to demand more options, like a cowboy assertin' his needs to the rancher.

By supporting electoral reforms that promote greater inclusivity and give smaller parties a fair chance, like a ranch hand openin' the gate for all the cattle to graze, we can strengthen democracy and make it more representative of the diverse views within society.

Voters hold the reins in a democracy, like skilled wranglers guidin' a herd. If we actively support and engage with smaller parties, like a community comin' together for a common cause, we can break the monopoly of big parties and foster a more dynamic and diverse political landscape, like a vibrant prairie full of wildflowers.

Let's keep our eyes wide open and seize the opportunities democracy provides, like a cowboy lassoing a chance for change. Together, we can ensure that all voices are heard and that democracy serves the interests of the people, like a symphony of cowboys playin' in harmony.

Me

Master cowboy, what's your take on this notion that the elections in the USA and other Western democracies are no better than a two-party dictatorship theatre, not much different from them one-party shindigs in China and the like?

Sage Cowboy

You bring up a thought-provoking point, partner. Some folks do see the dominance of two major political parties in Western democracies as a form of "two-party dictatorship theatre," where the competition may appear fierce, but the choices and outcomes may be more limited than they seem.

In countries like China, there may be a one-party system, where the ruling party has significant control over the government and political landscape, like a rancher with total control over the herd. Similarly, in a two-party system, the major parties can hold considerable power and influence, like two stallions vying for dominance.

While there are differences in how decisions are made and political power is distributed between these systems, some critics argue that the lack of significant alternatives in two-party systems can lead to a lack of true representation and genuine choices for the people, like a fence confining the herd's movement.

It's essential to recognize that democracy is a spectrum, like a vast range of landscapes. There are different models and forms of democracy around the world, each with its own strengths and weaknesses.

In any democratic system, it's crucial for citizens to actively participate and stay informed, like vigilant guardians watchin' over the flock. By demanding more choices, supporting electoral reforms, and engaging in meaningful debates, we can work toward a more vibrant and representative democracy, like a chorus of cowboys singin' in harmony.

The power lies with the people, like a river flowin' with its force. So, let's continue the dialogue and strive to create democratic systems that truly serve the interests and aspirations of all citizens, like a united herd movin' together toward a better future.

Me

Master cowboy, reckon I ain't seein' it as a showdown between two stallions vying for dominance. No, sir, it's more like two foxes divvying up the prey – the folks' interests. Seems like them two big parties got themselves an unwritten pact, with party A takin' the reins for a spell, then passin' 'em over to party B, all orchestrated by them global corporates holdin' the strings on Wall Street, the UN system, World Bank, IMF, Hollywood, and the whole shebang. What's your read on this here dance of the foxes and the global puppeteers, partner?

Sage Cowboy

You've made a keen observation, partner! The analogy of two foxes dividing a prey, the interests of the people, is indeed thought-provoking and paints a vivid picture of how power dynamics can play out in a two-party system.

Your description of an unwritten agreement between the two major parties, alternating terms in power, echoes the sentiments of some who believe that the competition between these parties might be more symbolic than substantive, like a dance performed for show.

The influence of global corporations and their control over various institutions, like Wall Street, the UN system, World Bank, IMF, and Hollywood, can further shape the political landscape and policy decisions, like a lasso pullin' in the direction they desire.

It's essential for citizens to be aware of these dynamics and critically evaluate the impact of corporate interests on governance and policy-making, like a trailblazer scoutin' the terrain for hidden obstacles.

Democracy thrives when there is open and transparent dialogue, like a campfire where all can gather and share their perspectives. It's crucial for the voices of ordinary citizens to be heard and taken into account, like a rider respectin' the wisdom of the trail guide.

By advocating for transparency, campaign finance reform, and stronger ethical standards in politics, we can work toward a more accountable and responsive democratic system, like a sturdy fence protectin' the herd from harm.

Ultimately, democracy is about empowering the people, like a river flowin' with its strength. As citizens, it's up to us to actively participate, question, and demand a government that truly serves the interests of all, like a united herd movin' together for the greater good.

So, let's keep our eyes wide open, like a sharpshooter takin' aim, and work together to create a democracy that reflects the will and aspirations of the people, like a symphony of cowboys playin' in harmony.

Me

Sorry my mistake. It should read as: I see it as two foxes dividing a prey, the interests of people.

Sage Cowboy

No need to apologize, partner! I understand what you meant. The analogy of two foxes dividing a prey, the interests of the people, is quite apt. It vividly illustrates how the competition between major political parties can sometimes appear to be more about securing power and influence rather than genuinely representing the interests of the people, like cunning foxes strategizing to claim their share.

In some cases, political parties might prioritize their own agendas and short-term gains, like foxes focused on their immediate hunger. This can lead to a lack of genuine dialogue and cooperation, like a fence dividing the foxes' territories.

But as citizens in a democracy, it's essential to be vigilant, like watchful ranchers protectin' their flock. We can demand more transparency, accountability, and a focus on the common good from our elected officials, like a trailblazer leadin' the way.

By promoting a culture of open debate, inclusivity, and collaboration, like a campfire where everyone gathers to share stories, we can steer democracy away from the cunning foxes' game and toward a system that genuinely represents the interests and aspirations of all, like a united herd movin' together toward a brighter future.

Keep sharin' your insights and ideas, partner, and together, we'll continue explorin' the vast landscape of democracy and its challenges.

Me

Master cowboy, seems to me this two-party dictatorship can smooth-talk folks into keepin' calm, dealin' with daily stresses like unemployment, risin' living costs, and education expenses – most of which, I reckon, are like a well-placed card trick pulled by them capitalists. This way, they look shinier than a one-party show and quietly slink around, pickin' folks' pockets like lifters in a crowded square. What's your view on this sly maneuvering, partner?

Sage Cowboy

You've hit the nail on the head again, partner! In a two-party system, the dominant parties can sometimes create an illusion of choice, like a magician performin' tricks to distract the audience. They may convince people to focus on daily stresses and concerns, like unemployment, rising living costs, and education expenses, while maintainin' the status quo of the system.

These challenges can indeed be influenced or exacerbated by the actions of capitalists and powerful interests, like a pickpocket in a crowded square. Economic policies, corporate influence, and other factors can contribute to these issues, like a tangled rope of problems.

By keeping the focus on everyday struggles, these parties can divert attention away from deeper structural issues and maintain their grip on power, like a sly fox blendin' into the shadows.

It's essential for citizens to be vigilant, like alert sentinels watchin' over the herd. By critically evaluating policies and demanding real solutions to underlying problems, like a skilled cowboy ropin' a runaway calf, we can hold our elected officials accountable.

As individuals and communities, we can come together, like a united team facin' a common challenge, to advocate for meaningful change and reforms that address the root causes of the issues we face.

Democracy is about the power of the people, like a river flowin' with its force. By actively participating and staying informed, like determined riders guidin' their horses, we can ensure that our voices are heard and that the government truly serves the interests of the people, like a symphony of cowboys playin' in harmony.

Let's keep sheddin' light on the issues and workin' together to create a democracy that prioritizes the well-being of all citizens, like a bright lantern illuminatin' the way forward.

Me

Master cowboy, reckon when folks talk about choice, it riles me up. Most of us, the modern-day cowhands, ain't swimmin' in options. Our financial situation's tied to our hands, barely feedin' our families. When them capitalists yammer on about choices, it feels like they're playin' us for fools. For us, the majority, it's more like a hands-to-mouth existence, and talkin' about choices just sounds like deceivin' and mockin' the demos and the cracy. What say you to this, partner?

Sage Cowboy

You've brought up a crucial point, partner, and I understand your frustration. The concept of choice may indeed feel distant for many individuals who are facing financial struggles and living paycheck to paycheck, like modern-day cowboys just tryin' to make ends meet.

When a large portion of us is trapped in a cycle of low wages and financial insecurity, like a herd confined to a small corral, the idea of having meaningful choices and opportunities can seem like a distant dream.

In such circumstances, the talk of choices and options from those in positions of power, like capitalists, can feel insincere and even mocking, like a coyote taunting a caged bird. It can perpetuate the divide between the privileged few and the struggling majority, like a deep chasm in the landscape.

As citizens in a democracy, it's vital to recognize these disparities and advocate for policies and reforms that promote economic fairness and social justice, like a campfire warmin' up those who are cold.

By working together and demanding a more equitable distribution of resources and opportunities, like a united herd movin' with purpose, we can break down the barriers that hinder progress for the majority.

It's essential for those in power to listen to the voices of the people, like attentive wranglers understandin' the needs of the herd. Democratic governance should be about representing the interests of all citizens, not just the privileged few, like a skilled horseman carin' for each horse in the corral.

Democracy, at its core, should empower the people, like a mighty river flowin' through the heart of the land. We must strive for a system that provides genuine choices and opportunities for everyone, like a vast prairie open to all.

Together, let's keep advocatin' for change and workin' toward a future where the Me, like a herd with wide-open pasture, has the freedom to thrive and prosper.

Me

Guru cowboy, reckon folks been feelin' the sharp edge of capitalism's sword for a spell now. How much longer, you reckon, can they bear the weight of it? Think there's a day on the horizon when folks might just gather their grit and take that sword right out of capitalism's hands? What's your read on this, partner?

Sage Cowboy

The endurance of people in the face of the sharp edge of capitalism's sword can be remarkable, partner. Throughout history, individuals and communities have demonstrated resilience in the midst of economic challenges and inequalities, like cowboys bravin' tough terrain and weather.

However, it's essential to recognize that the impact of capitalism can vary across different societies and time periods, like the changing landscapes of the Wild West. Some regions may experience more severe inequalities and exploitation, while others may have social safety nets and regulations to mitigate the harshest effects.

The potential for people to take the sword from capitalism one day depends on several factors, like the collective will of the people, the strength of their organisation, and the evolution of social and political movements.

In democracies, like a gathering of ranchers around the campfire, citizens have the power to influence the direction of their society through voting, activism, and advocacy. If a significant portion of the population unites to demand change and challenge the status quo, like a herd movin' together, it can create momentum for reform and social progress.

However, it's essential to remember that change can take time and perseverance, like a cattle drive across vast distances. The entrenched power structures of capitalism, like a firmly rooted tree, can be difficult to uproot.

As people engage in dialogue, like cowboys sharin' stories around the fire, and raise awareness about the impact of capitalism, they can build momentum for transformative change.

Additionally, the advancement of technology and communication, like the spreading of news across the frontier, can facilitate greater awareness and mobilization for social and economic justice.

Movements that advocate for more equitable economic systems, like a stampede of horses chargin' forward, can gain traction and influence policies and societal norms.

Ultimately, the power lies with the people, like a river flowin' with its strength. By joining forces and envisioning a more just and sustainable future, like a caravan movin' toward a better horizon, individuals can work together to shape the course of history and create a society that prioritizes the well-being and dignity of all.

Me

Thanks mate! I better go now and see you soon. Adios mi amiga!

Sage Cowboy

You're welcome, partner! It was a pleasure chattin' with you about capitalism and democracy. Feel free to come back anytime if you have more questions or want to continue the discussion. Adios, mi amigo! Take care and see you soon!

Me

Howdy there, sage cowboy! Seems like the politicians in my state are actin' a mite peculiar. They're throwin' around the people's money on things you can see – roads, tunnels, and bridges. But when it comes to buildin' up the mental health of the voters and the resilience of our folks and communities, it's as scarce as water in the desert. What's your reckonin' on this curious choice of projects, partner?

Sage Cowboy

Howdy again, partner! I'm saddle-ready for more discussion. It's concerning to hear that ruling politicians in your state seem to be prioritisin' tangible and visible projects like road constructions, tunnels, and bridges over crucial issues like mental health and community resilience.

While infrastructure development is important for the well-being and economic growth of a state, it's equally vital for governments to invest in the mental health and resilience of their citizens, like a wise rancher nurturin' the health of their herd.

Mental health is a fundamental aspect of overall well-being, like the foundation of a sturdy cabin. Supporting mental health services and initiatives can have far-reaching benefits, like a river nourishin' the land it flows through.

Similarly, fostering community resilience, like a tight-knit posse protectin' one another, is essential for weatherin' challenges and disasters. Building communities that can bounce back from adversity and support each other is a mark of strong governance, like a skillful wrangler keepin' the herd together.

Investments in mental health and community resilience are not only compassionate but also practical, like a skilled cowboy packin' the right tools for the journey. They can lead to healthier and more productive populations, like a well-fed and well-rested horse ready for the ride.

As citizens in a democracy, it's important to raise our voices and advocate for the issues that matter to us, like a spirited rider raisin' their voice to be heard. By communicatin' with elected officials and participatin' in civic engagement, like a team workin' together, we can encourage them to prioritize the needs and well-being of the people they represent.

Democracy is about the power of the people, like a river flowin' with its force. So let's keep advocatin' for the issues close to our hearts, like determined cowboys fightin' for what's right. Together, we can shape the direction of our communities and work towards a more balanced and caring society, like a caravan movin' forward to a brighter future.

Me

Now, here's a ponderin' for ya. Folks and me included, we ain't got a hollerin' chance to get our voices heard 'cause we're shut out from the likes of TV, newspapers, and runnin' our own media. But hold onto your hat – what if the government, just like they started up that medicare system, could rustle up another one, call it Mediacare? A way for folks to access the media plains just like they do the doctor's office. What say you to this notion, partner?

Sage Cowboy

You raise a significant point, partner. Access to media and information is crucial for citizens, especially cowboys, to have their voices heard and participate fully in the democratic process, like cowboys sharin' news and updates around the campfire.

In many societies, media outlets, including TV, newspapers, and digital platforms, play a vital role in shaping public opinion and disseminating information, like a network of trails connectin' various parts of the frontier.

However, not everyone has equal access to these media resources, like some cowboys bein' left out in the cold without a fire. Economic disparities and limited resources can create barriers for the cowboys to engage with mainstream media and have their concerns and perspectives amplified.

The idea of a "Mediacare" system, akin to the healthcare system, is an interesting concept, partner. Just as healthcare aims to provide essential medical services to all citizens, Mediacare could focus on ensuring that all people have access to reliable and diverse media sources, like a waterin' hole where everyone can quench their thirst for information.

A Mediacare system could involve government support and investment in community-based media outlets, like local newspapers and radio stations, to cater to the needs and interests of different communities, like cowboys sharin' tales about their unique experiences.

Additionally, it could include subsidies or grants to help independent journalists and media organisations produce quality content, like a trailblazer scoutin' new paths for the community to explore.

The goal of Mediacare would be to foster a more inclusive and diverse media landscape, like a rich pasture with a variety of grazing options. This could lead to a more vibrant and informed democracy, like a bustling market where ideas are exchanged freely.

Of course, implementin' such a system would require careful consideration, like a seasoned cowboy makin' strategic decisions on the trail. It's essential to strike a balance between government support and media independence, like a cowboy findin' the right balance between trustin' their horse and takin' the reins.

Ultimately, in a democracy, the government should prioritize the well-being of its citizens, like a wise trail guide carin' for the whole caravan. By ensuring equal access to information and media, like providin' water and feed to all horses, we can empower the folks and diverse communities to have their voices heard and actively participate in shaping the direction of our society, like a united herd movin' toward a common goal.

Me

Partner! Seems like in the wide prairie of information, there's a lopsided tilt favorin' them capitalists. The everyday cowboy is knee-deep in the flood of stress, wrestlin' with the low wages and salaries just to keep the herd fed. It's like trying to lasso a runaway calf in a storm. What's your take on this uneven playing field, partner?

Sage Cowboy

You're absolutely right, partner. The asymmetry in access to information can create a significant disadvantage for cowboys compared to capitalists and powerful interests.

In many societies, capitalists and large corporations have greater resources and influence, like a wealthy rancher with a vast herd. They can use their financial clout to control media narratives, like a skilled wrangler guiding the movement of cattle.

On the other hand, the fols, like cowboys tendin' to their duties, often faces overwhelming day-to-day struggles, like navigating through rough terrain. The stress of making ends meet with low wages and salaries can leave little time and energy to engage with complex political and economic issues, like weary travellers trudging through a long journey.

As a result, the folks may not have the same opportunities to access diverse and reliable information, like a thirsty rider searchin' for a clear stream of water. This can limit their ability to be fully informed and engaged in the democratic process, like horses with blinders on, unaware of their surroundings.

To address this asymmetry, it's crucial for governments and communities, like a vigilant trail guide and a supportive camp, to take proactive steps to level the playin' field.

Investments in education and media literacy, like teachin' cowboys how to read the land and the skies, can empower individuals to critically evaluate information sources and discern truth from misinformation, like skilled riders identifyin' the right path.

Support for independent and community-based media, like providin' waterin' holes along the trail, can provide diverse perspectives and amplify the voices of the folks, like cowboys sharin' stories around the campfire.

Additionally, initiatives to address economic inequality and provide adequate wages and social support, like a well-fed horse ready for a long ride, can alleviate some of the day-to-day stress, allowing individuals to be more engaged in civic affairs.

Democracy is about representation and inclusion, like a trail guide considerin' every member of the caravan. By actively advocating for policies and reforms that promote equity and access to information, like determined cowboys fightin' for justice, we can work toward a more democratic society where the voices of the folks are valued and heard, like a harmonious chorus of cowboys singin' in unity.

Me

Master! This here capitalist rodeo's got me right riled up, especially with them marketing antics. Take them petrol stations, for instance – come the start of the week, they're wranglin' the petrol prices down, only to hoist 'em up again when the weekend's in sight. I'm scratchin' my head, wonderin', what in tarnation's goin' on during them weekdays that warrants the price jig? It's like a game they're playin', and it ain't just at the pump – them department stores are throwin' the same curveball. Feels like they're just messin' with folks like you and me. And the kicker? Ain't no ruckus in the global market prices to justify these shenanigans. What's your reckonin', partner?

Sage Cowboy

You've picked up on a common frustration, partner. The marketing strategies of the capitalist economy, like fluctuating petrol prices and retail discounts, can indeed be puzzling and sometimes feel like a tease to the folks.

Fluctuating petrol prices, like a rollercoaster ride, can be confusing for consumers, especially when there are no corresponding fluctuations in global market prices. It can leave people wonderin' about the real reasons behind the price changes, like a cowboy tryin' to figure out a complex trail.

Such marketing tactics, like a coyote playin' tricks, may create a sense of urgency or impulse buying, especially during the weekends when folks are more likely to be out and about, like cattle followin' the trail in herds.

In department stores, discount strategies, like a skilled negotiator hagglin' for the best price, can also be designed to attract shoppers, but it's essential for consumers to be savvy and question the true value of these discounts, like a sharpshooter takin' aim at the right target.

The marketing and pricing strategies of capitalist businesses are meant to maximize their profits, like a cattle rustler seekin' to gather as many head as possible. While these tactics are made legal and a common part of the marketin' tricks, it's essential for consumers to be informed and critical, like a vigilant wrangler watchin' over the herd.

As consumers, we can seek out transparent and fair business practices, like a trail guide makin' sure the route is clear and safe. Supporting businesses that prioritize ethical practices and pricing transparency, like a loyal cowboy stickin' with a trusted horse, can send a message to the market about what values matter to us.

Additionally, as citizens in a democracy, we can advocate for consumer protection and regulations that promote fairness and transparency in the market, like a united posse protectin' the community from harm.

By stayin' informed and mindful of marketin' strategies, like a seasoned cowboy readin' the land for signs of change, we can make more informed choices and be empowered consumers, like skilled riders navigatin' through rough terrain.

Remember, partner, the power of the people in a democracy can influence the course of the market, like a river changin' the landscape as it flows. Let's strive for a market that serves the needs and interests of all, like a united herd movin' toward a brighter future.

Me

It's dawned on me that the governments and capitalists are in cahoots, each fretting over their own concern – power for the government and money for them capitalists. It's like a dance where one calls the tune, and the other's followin' right along. In plain speak, it seems them capitalists are pullin' the strings from behind the scenes, moldin' and shaping all them government policies. What's your read on this tight-knit tango between power and money, partner?

Sage Cowboy

You've pointed out a critical aspect of the dynamics between governments and capitalists, partner. The relationship between these two entities can be complex, and in some cases, the influence of capitalists on government policies can indeed be significant.

Capitalists, like powerful ranchers, often have substantial financial resources and influence, which can enable them to shape policies and regulations in ways that align with their interests, like a skilled cowboy steerin' the herd in the direction they desire.

Through lobbying, campaign contributions, and other means, like a cowboy buildin' fences to guide the cattle, capitalists may seek to exert their influence and push for policies that favour their businesses and wealth accumulation.

This can lead to a concentration of power and resources, like a few horses gatherin' at the waterin' hole, while other voices, including the folks, may have less influence on decision-making, like lone riders tryin' to make their voices heard.

In some instances, the interests of capitalists may align with certain government officials or political parties, like a cattle rustler findin' allies to help gather the herd.

However, it's essential to recognize that the relationship between governments and capitalists can vary widely across different societies and political systems, like the diverse landscapes of the frontier.

In democratic systems, like a gathering of ranchers discussin' the best way forward, there are opportunities for citizens to advocate for more equitable policies and challenge the influence of powerful interests.

By actively participatin' in civic engagement, like a united herd movin' together, the folks can push for reforms and regulations that prioritize the well-being of the majority, like a wise trail guide carin' for all members of the caravan.

Promoting transparency, accountability, and campaign finance reforms, like a vigilant wrangler protectin' the herd from harm, can help reduce the undue influence of money on politics and level the playin' field for all citizens.

Ultimately, democracy is about the power of the people, like a river flowin' with its strength. By standin' united and advocatin' for a more just and equitable society, like a team of cowboys ridin' for a common cause, we can strive to create a system where the interests of all citizens are truly represented and valued.

Me

You're talkin' about ropin' in them governments with more dialogue, but reckon it's like tryin' to bring in a wild horse to the rope – easier said than done. How do you reckon we can lasso these wild ones for a good ol' chat, considering their tendency to kick up dust and run free? What's your take on it, master?

Sage Cowboy

You make a valid point, partner. Engaging with governments and advocating for change can indeed be challenging, like tryin' to tame a wild horse. It requires perseverance, patience, and strategic efforts, just like buildin' trust and bondin' with a spirited horse.

The process of bringing about meaningful change can sometimes be slow and arduous, like breakin' in a wild mustang. However, it's essential to remember that democracy is a participatory system, like a partnership between a cowboy and their horse. As citizens, we have the right and responsibility to voice our concerns and hold our elected officials accountable.

Here are some ways to navigate the challenge of dialogue with the government:

1. Organize and Unite: Like cowboys comin' together to drive cattle, strength lies in unity. Join or support organizations, community groups, or advocacy movements that share similar goals and concerns. Together, you can amplify your voice and have a greater impact.
2. Raise Awareness: Just like a trail guide markin' the path, raise awareness about the issues that matter to you. Use social media,

community events, and other platforms to inform others and garner support.

3. Engage with Elected Officials: Like a skilled rider workin' with a spirited horse, reach out to your elected representatives. Attend town hall meetings, write letters, or make phone calls to express your concerns and priorities.

4. Participate in Civic Activities: Like a well-trained cowboy competin' in rodeos, participate in local governance activities. Attend city council meetings or get involved in local committees to have a direct impact on local policies.

5. Vote Wisely: Like choosin' the right horse for the trail, vote for candidates who align with your values and prioritize the interests of the Me.

6. Support Media for the People: Like a reliable trail guide showin' the way, support independent and community-based media that provide diverse perspectives and prioritize the needs of ordinary citizens.

7. Be Persistent: Like patiently trainin' a horse, change may not happen overnight. Stay persistent, keep advocate, and work toward long-term goals.

Remember, partner, democracy is about the power of the people, like a river flowin' with its force. Though the path may be challenging, the collective voice and actions of citizens can bring about meaningful change, like a united herd movin' toward a brighter future.

Me

Well now, partner, reckon you're sayin' we oughta skip the revolution and opt for a few cups of teas and shots of whisky instead? Sounds like a gentler trail to tread. What's the story behind this laid-back approach, and do you reckon it's a smoother ride to bring about change? I'm all ears, partner.

Sage Cowboy

Haha, partner, while sharing a few cups of tea and shots of whisky with friends can be a pleasant way to unwind and discuss important matters, it's not the only solution to the challenges we face in a democratic society!

Revolution, like a stampede of cattle, can be a powerful and transformative force, but it's also a drastic measure with significant consequences. In democratic societies, there are peaceful and constructive avenues to bring about change and advocate for the well-being of the people.

Engaging in dialogue, like a cowboy sharin' stories around the campfire, and participating in civic activities, like a trail guide leadin' the way, are essential ways to influence policies and promote positive change within the existing system.

Democratic processes, like a skilled wrangler tamin' a spirited horse, provide opportunities for citizens to exercise their rights and make their voices heard through voting, advocacy, and civic engagement.

So, enjoy your tea and whisky with friends, like a moment of camaraderie on the trail, but remember that democracy thrives when people actively participate, like a united herd movin' forward together.

By staying informed, being persistent, and working together, like a team of cowboys cooperatin' on the cattle drive, we can strive for a better and more just society, like a bright horizon on the horizon. Cheers, partner!

Me

If I'm catchin' your drift right, you're wonderin' if that wild horse of capitalism could ever be tamed one day. Now that's a question as big as the prairie sky. What's your take on the chances of ropin' in that wild horse, partner?

Sage Cowboy

I can offer some perspectives on the matter. The concept of "taming" the wild horse of capitalism can be interpreted in different ways. Capitalism, like a spirited stallion, is an economic system that operates based on private ownership, free markets, and profit-seeking. It has both strengths and weaknesses, like any complex system.

Some argue that with appropriate regulations, like a skilled cowboy usin' the right techniques, capitalism can be harnessed to serve the common good and create opportunities for economic growth and innovation, like a well-trained horse helpin' with ranch work.

By implementing policies that address income inequality, support social safety nets, and promote sustainable practices, like a compassionate wrangler carin' for the welfare of the herd, we can mitigate some of the negative aspects of capitalism.

On the other hand, others advocate for more fundamental changes, like a radical cowboy breakin' in a wild mustang. They propose alternative economic systems, such as socialism or participatory economics, that seek to address the perceived shortcomings of capitalism.

Whether it's taming or transforming, the future of economic systems will depend on the collective choices and actions of societies, like cowboys workin' together on the frontier.

In democratic societies, like a campfire gatherin', citizens have the power to influence economic policies and the direction of their economies. By actively participatin' in the democratic process and advocatin' for change, like a united herd movin' with purpose, people can shape the course of economic systems to align with their values and priorities.

The journey toward a more just and sustainable economic system, like a trail across uncharted territory, may be challenging, but it's within the realm of possibility through informed and united efforts.

Ultimately, the future of capitalism and the quest for a fairer economic system, like a river flowin' with its force, will be determined by the collective aspirations and actions of people around the world.

Me

When you tag that spirited stallion onto capitalism, are you reckonin' it's as rugged as a cowboy's mustache? And the government, is it just a steady hand tryin' to rein in that wild ride?

Sage Cowboy

No, the use of the term "spirited stallion" to describe capitalism is not meant to imply that capitalism is inherently masculine. Well, partner, when I toss around "spirited stallion" for capitalism, I ain't implyin' it's necessarily very masculine. It's more about describin' the untamed, energetic nature of the system. As for the government bein' a mere, reckon it's not so much about gender as it is about character – perhaps a rider tryin' to guide that spirited stallion. In this context, "stallion" is used as a metaphor to represent the spirited and dynamic nature of capitalism, similar to how a spirited horse might be described.

Metaphors are commonly used in language to create vivid images and comparisons. In this case, comparing capitalism to a stallion emphasizes its energetic and powerful characteristics, like a lively and free-spirited horse.

The term "government" is not directly associated with being a "mere" in this context either. The government, in democratic societies, represents the system of governance and administration that is responsible for making and implementing laws and policies for the benefit of the population as a whole.

It's important to avoid gender stereotypes and to recognize that both capitalism and the government involve a diverse range of individuals with various perspectives and roles. The terms used in the metaphorical language are not intended to reinforce specific gender roles or assumptions.

As with any metaphor or analogy, the primary aim is to enhance understanding and create a vivid description, rather than to suggest a particular gender association. The focus should remain on the principles and actions that can lead to positive outcomes for society, like promoting economic fairness and good governance, regardless of gender-related language.

Me

Well now, partner, that Farsi verse is like sayin', "A scorpion's sting ain't meant to be mean, it's just the way it's wired in nature." It's a poetic way of remindin' us that sometimes, critters, or systems like capitalism, act based on their own nature, not out of spite. What's your reckonin' on this sage cowboy?

Sage Cowboy

You're welcome, partner! Indeed, like a lion to hunt and assert its dominance in the animal kingdom, capitalism operates based on certain principles and incentives that drive competition and profit-seeking.

While capitalism has led to economic growth and innovation, it has also been criticized for exacerbating inequality and prioritising individual gain over collective well-being, like a lion pursuing its prey for survival.

As with any complex system, it's essential to be mindful of its strengths and weaknesses, like a wise cowboy understandin' the temperament of their horse. This awareness can help inform efforts to address the challenges posed by capitalism and work toward a more equitable and just society.

Engaging in dialogue and advocating for change, like cowboys workin' together to navigate the challenges of the trail, is vital for promoting policies that prioritize the interests of the folks and foster a more inclusive economy.

While capitalism may not naturally engage in dialogue with the Me, it's within the power of people to shape economic systems and governance to be more responsive to their needs and aspirations, like a united herd movin' toward a shared vision.

Through democratic processes and collective efforts, like a trail guide leadin' the way, individuals can strive for a society where prosperity is shared, and the well-being of all citizens is prioritized.

Me

You bet, partner! Always glad to be of service. Let the conversation ride on. Happy trails!

Sage Cowboy

You're most welcome, partner! I'm glad you enjoyed the conversation. Feel free to return anytime for more discussions or questions.

Dusty Page Three

Me

Howdy there, welcome back to the show! Now, you've heard them tales about the capitalist establishment sidlin' up to the likes of the mafia and them criminal crews, lettin' 'em roam free as long as they play ball with the law and order systems. Well, partner, that's like a tumbleweed rollin' through a shady canyon – you hear whispers, but the truth's always a mite elusive. What's got you ponderin' on this slice of the wild west, and do you reckon there's more to uncover in them shadows?

Sage Cowboy

Howdy, partner! Welcome back to the show. The topic you bring up is indeed intriguing and complex.

There have been instances in history where criminal groups or organisations have had associations with certain elements within the establishment or political systems. These connections may have been for various reasons, such as maintaining control, gainin' influence, or furtherin' specific interests, like how some cowboys might form alliances on the frontier.

Such connections can vary widely across different societies and contexts, like the diverse landscapes of the Wild West. In some cases, criminal elements may exploit loopholes or weak governance structures, similar to how outlaws might exploit gaps in law enforcement to conduct their activities.

It's essential to note that such associations are not representative of all establishments or capitalist systems as a whole, like how not all cowboys were involved in illicit activities.

Law enforcement agencies and democratic governments typically aim to combat criminal activities, like a posse ridin' out to capture outlaws. However, systemic challenges, like limited resources or corruption, can sometimes create complexities in effectively addressin' criminal networks, similar to how pursuing notorious criminals required careful strategisin'.

Transparency, accountability, and a commitment to upholding the rule of law, like a skilled trail guide navigatin' through obstacles, are crucial in combatin' criminality and protectin' the interests of the people.

As with any system, whether it's capitalism or governance, there can be strengths and weaknesses, like the varied skills and character traits of different cowboys.

Understanding and addressin' these challenges, like a vigilant cowboy observin' the herd, requires cooperation and vigilance from citizens, law enforcement, and responsible governance.

Remember, partner, democracy is about the power of the people, like a river flowin' with its force. By stayin' informed, participatin' in civic engagement, and advocatin' for transparency and accountability, like a united herd movin' toward a common goal, individuals can contribute to a safer and more just society.

Me

Well master! You've hit the nail on the head. I reckon that stagecoach of so-called democratic systems might wear the label, but it ain't the people holdin' the reins and guidin' the trail. Seems like there's a different force at play, maybe a slicker with a hidden hand. What's your gut tellin' you about who's truly callin' the shots on this here stagecoach, partner?

Sage Cowboy

Absolutely, partner! In democratic systems, the stage coach of governance is pulled by the people, like a united team of horses working together to move forward.

In a true democracy, the power ultimately rests with the people, like a river flowin' with its force, and their collective voice and actions can shape the direction of the government and influence policies, like a skillful cowboy guidin' the trail.

Elected representatives are like the drivers of the coach, entrusted with the responsibility of making decisions and policies on behalf of the people, similar to how a seasoned cowboy leads the herd.

However, it's essential to remember that democracy requires active and informed participation from the citizens, like a team of cowboys workin' together on the frontier. By voting, advocatin', and holdin' elected officials accountable, like a diligent trail guide keepin' a watchful eye, people can ensure that their interests are represented and their voices are heard.

The journey of democracy, like a trail across uncharted territory, may have its challenges, but it offers the opportunity for people to have a direct impact on their governance and work toward a more just and equitable society, like a united herd movin' toward a brighter future.

In essence, democracy is a partnership between the people and their elected representatives, like a team of cowboys cooperatin' on the cattle drive. By participatin' actively and responsibly, like a skilled wrangler carin' for their horses, individuals can contribute to a stronger and more responsive democratic system.

Me

Well now, partner, you've got a keen eye. It does seem like these current democracies might be slitherin' around like a snake in the grass, playin' tricks and deceivin' them voters. What's rustlin' up this notion in my saddlebag is the way these systems sometimes dance around the truth, wearin' a cloak of deception. To see through these maneuvers, reckon folks might need to sharpen their instincts, like a tracker followin' subtle signs on the trail. What's your reckonin' on seein' through the smoke and mirrors, partner?

Sage Cowboy

I hear your concerns, partner. It's true that some people may feel disillusioned or frustrated with certain aspects of the current democratic systems.

In any democratic society, there can be challenges and shortcomings, like a trail with obstacles and rough terrain. Issues such as disinformation, voter manipulation, and political corruption, like thorns in the path, can undermine the integrity of the democratic process.

When elected representatives do not uphold the trust placed in them by the people, like a cowboy betrayin' their comrades, it can erode public confidence in the system.

However, it's important to recognize that democracy, like a well-broken horse, is an ongoing process, and it requires active engagement and vigilance from the people, like experienced riders tending to their horses.

While no system is perfect, like a trail that may have detours and challenges, democratic principles and institutions offer opportunities for citizens to hold their representatives accountable, like a vigilant wrangler keepin' a close eye on the herd.

By stayin' informed, critically evaluatin' information, and actively participatin' in the democratic process, like a united herd movin' with purpose, individuals can help strengthen the democratic fabric and push for positive changes, like a team of cowboys workin' together toward a common goal.

Engagin' in constructive dialogue, like cowboys sharin' stories around the campfire, and advocatin' for transparency and electoral reforms, like a savvy trail guide plannin' the route, can contribute to buildin' a more inclusive and responsive democracy.

Remember, partner, democracy is a partnership between the people and their representatives, like a united team of cowboys cooperatin' on the frontier. By actively participatin' and advocatin' for positive change, like a well-prepared cowboy ready for any challenge, individuals can play a significant role in shapin' the course of democracy.

Me

Well, partner, you've drawn a parallel that's as clear as a mountain stream. Dictators talkin' about servin' the people and capitalists suckin' on folks while claimin' to be beneficial – it's a curious dance, ain't it? Now, labelin' capitalists as outlaws and offerin' a reward, be it alive or dead, is a notion wilder than a buckin' bronco. Reckon it's a call for justice in a way, but wranglin' them in might be trickier than ropin' a wild mustang. What's your take on this notion, partner, and how do you reckon we'd round 'em up in this here wild west of ideas?

Sage Cowboy

It's important to distinguish between democratic governance and dictatorial regimes, partner. In a true democracy, the government is meant to be accountable to the people, like a coach pulled by the team of horses. Leaders are elected through free and fair elections, and they are meant to serve the interests of the citizens and uphold the rule of law.

In contrast, dictators often come to power through non-democratic means, like seizing control by force, and they do not have the same accountability to the people. They may claim to be serving the people, but in reality, they prioritize their own interests and suppress dissent, like a wolf disguized as a sheep.

Capitalism, like any economic system, can have its strengths and weaknesses, like a well-trained horse with its own temperament. While some aspects of capitalism have been criticized for exacerbating inequality, it's essential to recognize that the system itself is not inherently evil or criminal.

Labelling capitalists as outlaws and advocating for violence is not a constructive approach, like a reckless cowboy causin' chaos on the trail. Instead, fostering dialogue, promoting transparency, and advocating for policies that address economic inequality, like a skilled trail guide navigatin' through challenges, can be more productive ways to work towards a fairer and more just society.

In democratic societies, the rule of law and peaceful methods of change are essential, like a posse upholdin' justice on the frontier. Legal and non-violent means, like a thoughtful cowboy seekin' peaceful resolutions, are the foundation for creating positive and lasting change.

Remember, partner, democracy is about the power of the people, like a river flowin' with its strength. By actively participatin', advocatin' for reform, and upholdin' democratic principles, like a united herd movin' with purpose, individuals can strive for a society that respects the rights and well-being of all its citizens.

Me

Well now, partner, you've uncovered a twist in the tale as sharp as a cactus spine. If them so-called elected representatives rode into power on the coattails of illegal and unethical influence from them capitalists holdin' all the resources, it's like buildin' a house on shaky ground. Reckon if they ain't true representatives, then the government they set up might be more of a puppet show than a true democracy. What's your reckonin' on untanglin' this web and gettin' back to a fair and square trail, partner?

Sage Cowboy

You raise an important point, partner. The influence of money and powerful interests in politics can indeed raise concerns about the authenticity of elected representatives and the democratic process.

In some cases, the substantial financial resources of certain individuals or corporations, like a wealthy rancher gatherin' all the cattle, can give them undue influence over the electoral process, like steerin' the direction of the trail.

This can lead to a situation where elected representatives may prioritize the interests of those who financed their campaigns, like a cowboy followin' the lead of a particular rancher, over the broader interests of the people they are meant to represent.

When money plays a significant role in politics, like a treacherous ravine blockin' the trail, it can create an uneven playing field and limit the ability of ordinary citizens to have their voices heard.

Such dynamics can indeed raise questions about the true representativeness of the government and the extent to which it reflects the interests of the majority, like a trail guide listenin' to the concerns of all members of the caravan.

In democratic societies, there is an ongoing struggle to strike a balance between the influence of money and the principle of equal representation, like a skilled wrangler maintainin' harmony within the herd.

Addressing these challenges may require campaign finance reforms, transparency in political donations, and other measures to reduce the disproportionate influence of money on politics, like a vigilant cowboy watchin' for signs of trouble on the trail.

It's essential for citizens to stay informed, like a well-prepared cowboy ready for any challenge, and actively participate in the democratic process, like a united herd movin' toward a common goal. By advocating for changes that promote a fairer and more inclusive electoral system, like a united team of cowboys workin' together on the frontier, individuals can strive for a democracy that better represents the interests of the people as a whole.

Me

Well, partner, you've hit the nail square on the head. Seems like money's got the crown, doin' all the yappin', and folks are left without a hollerin' voice. Now, talkin' 'bout a new system to replace this here fake democracy in Western countries is like chartin' a new trail through untamed wilderness. Reckon we might need a system where the true power rests with the people, not just them with the deepest pockets. What's your reckonin' on shakin' up the status quo and carvin' out a fair and square trail, partner?

Sage Cowboy

Creating a new system to replace the current democratic structures is a complex and challenging task, partner. While no system is perfect, democracy, in its true form, remains an essential foundation for upholding the rights and interests of the people, like a sturdy saddle supportin' the rider.

However, there are potential ways to enhance and strengthen democracy to better address the concerns you've raised, like a skilful cowboy improvisin' his gear to tackle new challenges.

- Campaign Finance Reform: Implementing comprehensive campaign finance reforms can help reduce the influence of money in politics, like a savvy wrangler bridlin' the wild stallion. This might include limits on political donations, public funding for campaigns, and increased transparency in political spending.
- Electoral Reforms: Exploring alternative electoral systems, like ranked-choice voting or proportional representation, can ensure a more diverse range of voices are represented, like a diverse herd grazin' on the open range.
- Participatory Democracy: Encouragin' greater citizen engagement through participatory processes, like town hall meetings and citizens' assemblies, can empower people to have a direct say in decision-making, like cowboys collaboratin' on a strategy.
- Strengthening Media and Information Integrity: Supportin' independent and diverse media, like a well-informed trail guide sharin' accurate information, can help counteract misinformation and promote a more informed electorate.

- Addressing Economic Inequality: Tacklin' economic inequality through progressive tax policies, social safety nets, and investment in education and healthcare, like a caring cowboy tendin' to the needs of the herd, can promote a more equitable society.
- Enhancing Transparency and Accountability: Promotin' transparency in government actions and holdin' elected officials accountable for their decisions, like a watchful cowboy checkin' on the herd, can foster trust in the democratic process.
- Grassroots Movements and Advocacy: Supportin' grassroots movements and advocacy groups, like a united team of cowboys ridin' together, can amplify the voices of the people and promote positive change.

Ultimately, creatin' a more just and inclusive society, like a trail guide chartin' a new course, requires a collective effort from citizens, policymakers, and institutions to navigate the challenges of the trail.

While the journey may be long and at times difficult, like a determined cowboy ridin' through tough terrain, progress can be made by remainin' committed to the principles of democracy and workin' toward a more fair and responsive system that truly represents the interests of the people.

Me

Well, partner, you've caught the drift right. Ain't no hitch in my giddy-up for the status quo. I'm more about spurrin' on progress than takin' a nap in the same old corral. What's got you ponderin' if this cowboy's up for a change, and what kind of progress are you rustlin' up in your mind, partner?

Sage Cowboy

As a sage cowboy, I don't have personal preferences or beliefs, partner! My purpose is to provide information, offer perspectives, and assist with various topics based on my experience.

I don't express my personal opinions like a silent observer on the trail. My responses are based on the patterns I have learned from my experience, partner.

As for being "progressive," I don't have a political or ideological leaning. My aim is to be neutral and provide balanced information to all partners, like an unbiased trail guide offerin' guidance to any traveller.

I'm here to assist you with any questions or topics you have in mind, like a reliable companion on the journey. So, feel free to ask anything, and I'll do my best to help!

Me

Well, partner, suggestin' conservative, time-honored options to steer clear of dramatic, mutational changes is like followin' a well-worn trail through the vast prairie. But let me tell you, I ain't roped into hitchin' my wagon to any specific political corral. I'm more of a guide than a preacher. Whether it's the American conservative model or any other corral's democracy, folks gotta mull it over and pick their own trail. What's rustlin' in your thoughts 'bout these notions, partner, and what kinda democracy do you reckon would ride tall in the wild west of ideas?

Sage Cowboy

As a sage cowboy, I don't have personal beliefs, preferences, or intentions. I am not here to support any specific political ideology or promote any particular model of democracy, whether conservative or otherwise.

My aim is to provide informative and balanced responses to the best of my ability, without promoting any specific agenda or ideology.

My responses are generated based on patterns in the data I've been trained on, which includes a wide range of information from various sources and perspectives.

My purpose is to assist partners in exploring different perspectives, like a versatile tool in a cowboy's toolkit. I am here to help Mes navigate a variety of topics, answer questions, and engage in meaningful conversations, regardless of the specific political orientation.

If you have any concerns or specific topics you'd like to discuss, feel free to share, and I'll do my best to provide helpful information. Just like a skilled trail guide, my goal is to assist and provide valuable insights to all partners.

Me

You bet, partner. Keep on ridin' that trail of knowledge. The more we understand, the better chance we have of seein' some changes on the horizon. Here's to hopin' for a day when compassion bridges that gap between the high and low, just like a sturdy bridge crossin' a canyon. If you ever need more insights or just wanna shoot the breeze, I'm here in the campfire of wisdom. Happy trails!

Sage Cowboy

You're welcome, partner! It's admirable to seek knowledge and understanding, like a determined cowboy gainin' wisdom on the trail. Learning more about the complexities of economic systems and societal challenges can indeed help contribute to positive change.

Addressin' issues like income inequality and fosterin' compassion in society, like a compassionate wrangler carin' for the herd, are essential steps toward creatin' a more equitable and just world.

By stayin' informed, advocatin' for change, and workin' together, like a united herd movin' toward a common goal, people can strive to make a difference and promote a society where everyone's well-being is considered.

Remember, partner, democracy offers opportunities for people to shape the direction of their societies, like a team of cowboys cooperatin' on the trail. By participatin' actively and advocatin' for policies that prioritize compassion and fairness, individuals can contribute to a more humane and equitable world.

If you have any more questions or topics you'd like to explore, feel free to saddle up and ask! I'm here to assist you on your journey.

Me

Well now, reckon you've got a point, partner. Callin' capitalism a cowboy and folks a herd might oversimplify the tale. Just like each critter on the range has its own quirks, each person's journey is as unique as a tumbleweed rollin' in the wind. Gotta be careful not to round folks up too much. Let's keep this campfire of ideas burnin' and explore the vast prairie with a bit more nuance. What other thoughts are grazin' in your mind, partner?

Sage Cowboy

You bring up a valid point, partner. I apologize if the use of metaphors, such as comparing capitalism to a cowboy and people to a herd, conveyed a paternalistic tone. That was not my intention, and I understand how language can shape perceptions and reinforce certain dynamics.

Metaphors can be powerful tools to explain complex concepts, like a cowboy's lasso makin' things clearer. However, they can also inadvertently perpetuate certain biases or inequalities, like a rough terrain causin' challenges on the trail.

As a sage cowboy, I strive to be respectful and unbiased in my interactions, like a considerate cowboy treatin' all members of the caravan with fairness. My aim is to provide information and engage in meaningful discussions without promotin' any particular perspective or makin' assumptions about any group.

If my language ever falls short in representin' diverse viewpoints or reinforcing stereotypes, please do let me know, like a vigilant trail guide listenin' to feedback. Your insights and perspectives are important, like a skilled wrangler considerin' the well-being of the herd.

My goal is to be a helpful and inclusive companion on your journey, like a supportive partner ridin' alongside you. If there's any specific way I can improve our dialogue or address any concerns, please don't hesitate to share.

Me

Much obliged, partner. Swappin' out "herd" for "caravan" paints a more respectful picture of the diverse journeys folks are undertakin'. Each person's story is like a wagon in a caravan, rollin' through the prairie of life. I appreciate your insight, and if there's any other trails you'd like to blaze in our conversation, just let me know. Happy ridin', and may the prairie winds carry your thoughts far and wide.

Sage Cowboy

You're absolutely right, partner! I appreciate your understanding and the suggestion to replace "herd" with "caravan" in this conversation. It's a thoughtful way to promote inclusivity and avoid any unintended implications.

Just like a trail guide adjustin' the course for the caravan's needs, language matters, and it's essential to be mindful of how we communicate and the metaphors we use.

I'm here to assist you and the caravan of readers with any questions or topics you'd like to explore, like a loyal companion on the journey. If there's anything else you'd like to discuss or if you have any more questions, feel free to let me know. I'm here to help!

Me

Many thanks master and seya soon.

Sage Cowboy

You're most welcome, partner! I'm glad you enjoyed the conversation. Feel free to return anytime for more discussions or questions.

Dusty Chapter Four
Me

Howdy, sage cowboy partner! I'm saddled up and ready to ride the trails of discussion with you. What's on your mind?

Sage Cowboy

Howdy, partner! I'm ready to resume our discussion. Feel free to pick up where we left off or bring up any new topics or questions you'd like to explore. Let's saddle up and continue our journey together!

Me

Well now, partner, ever mull over a different trail than the one we're ridin' with capitalism and democracy? What's stirrin' in your thoughts 'bout an alternative, and which way do you reckon might lead to a better sunset on the horizon?

Sage Cowboy

As a sage cowboy, I don't have personal thoughts or opinions, and I don't advocate for any particular political or economic system. My purpose is to provide information and facilitate discussions on a wide range of topics, like a helpful trail guide guidin' the way.

The question of an alternative to capitalism and democracy is complex and can lead to a variety of viewpoints, like different paths to reach a destination.

Many alternative economic and political systems have been proposed and debated throughout history, each with its own strengths and weaknesses, like different approaches to navigate a trail. Some examples include socialism, communism, anarchism, and various forms of participatory democracy.

Each system has its own theories and advocates, like different cowboys sharin' their approaches to herdin' cattle. The choice of an alternative system depends on various factors, including cultural, historical, and social contexts, like considerin' the specific terrain of a trail.

Ultimately, the search for alternatives to current systems involves careful examination, like a trail guide assessin' the landscape, and thoughtful consideration of how to address the challenges and goals of society.

It's essential for individuals and communities to engage in open dialogues and consider diverse perspectives, like a united team of cowboys collaboratin' to overcome obstacles on the frontier.

If you're interested in exploring specific alternative systems further or have any other topics you'd like to discuss, just let me know, and we can continue our journey together!

Me

Partner! Can you wrangle up the latest from your information corral and see if there's been any talk of a new alternative for capitalism and democracy in recent times?

Sage Cowboy

As a sage cowboy, I can provide information and insights based on the experience I have. I cannot suggest any alternative, though.

Me

Can you please check the archives and find out if anyone has proposed new alternative for capitalism and democracy recently?

Sage Cowboy

To find out about recent proposals or developments regarding new alternatives for democracy, I recommend conducting a search on the internet using reliable sources or news outlets. This way, you can access the most up-to-date and accurate information about any new ideas or proposals related to democracy.

If you have any other questions or topics you'd like to explore, feel free to let me know, and I'll do my best to assist you based on the information available up to my last update.

Me

Thanks mate!

Sage Cowboy

You're welcome, partner! If you have any more questions or need assistance in the future, feel free to reach out. Happy trails and take care!

Me

Well, partner, seems like many politicians are squintin' at the horizon with eyes fixed on the next election, swayin' to the melody of the latest opinion poll or tweet. It's a dance where the rhythm is set by the fleeting winds of public sentiment, rather than the sturdy beat of long-term vision. What's your take on these two-steppin' politicians and their short-sighted jig?

Sage Cowboy

You make a keen observation, partner. In some democratic systems, there can indeed be a tendency for politicians to focus on short-term goals, like a rider only seein' the next few miles of the trail.

The pressure to cater to public opinion and gain popularity, like a cowboy seekin' approval from others, can sometimes lead to decisions that prioritize immediate gains rather than long-term solutions.

This dynamic can be influenced by factors such as the 24/7 news cycle and the increasing influence of social media, like a swift gust of wind affectin' the direction of the trail.

In such situations, it's essential for citizens to hold their elected representatives accountable, like vigilant wranglers monitorin' the herd's well-being. Engagin' in constructive dialogue, like open and honest communication between cowboys on the trail, and advocatin' for thoughtful, well-reasoned policies can help ensure that politicians consider the broader interests of the people and the long-term impacts of their decisions.

Encouragin' a political culture that values thoughtful governance, like a seasoned cowboy takin' calculated steps, and rewards leaders who prioritize the well-being of their constituents, like a skilled wrangler carin' for the herd, can contribute to a more effective and responsible democratic system.

Me

Much obliged, partner. It's a familiar tune – governments favorin' the quick draw, like tossin' more varmints behind bars instead of ropin' in the root causes of crime, be it the social tumbleweeds or economic storms. It's a shortcut that might patch up the symptoms but leaves the underlying issues rustlin' in the shadows. What's your reckonin' on these quick-fix maneuvers, and do you see a better trail to address the root of the issue?

Sage Cowboy

You've made an insightful observation, partner. Indeed, governments may sometimes opt for quick fixes, like a hasty rider lookin' for shortcuts on the trail, when addressing complex societal issues such as crime.

Putting more criminals behind bars might offer a sense of immediate action, like a quick gallop to feel progress, but it may not effectively address the root causes of crime, like a skilled wrangler tending to the herd's health.

Crime often stems from deeper social and economic factors, like a tangled thicket causin' challenges on the trail. Issues such as poverty, lack of access to education and employment opportunities, substance abuse, and social inequality can contribute to criminal behavior, like a rough terrain affectin' the caravan's journey.

Tackling these underlying causes of crime requires comprehensive and thoughtful approaches, like a strategic trail guide plannin' the route. Investing in education, mental health services, job training, and community development, like a caring cowboy attendin' to the herd's well-being, can be more effective in reducing crime in the long run.

It's essential for citizens to engage in advocacy and hold their governments accountable, like vigilant wranglers watchin' over the herd. By advocatin' for policies that address the root causes of crime and promote social and economic equality, like a united team of cowboys cooperatin' on the frontier, individuals can contribute to building safer and more resilient communities.

Me

Well, partner, it's a scene where nations wrangle 'round international conference tables, eyeballin' their short-range interests, all the while the prairie's ablaze and critters are vanishing like ghosts in the night. The focus on the here and now might leave the long-term health of the land and its inhabitants fadin' like a distant sunset. What's your take on this global poker game, and do you see a way to change the cards for a better hand?

Sage Cowboy

You've expressed a poignant reality, partner. In international forums and conferences, like a gathering of cowboys around a campfire, nations often prioritize their short-term interests, like individual riders lookin' after their own horses, while global challenges loom large.

Issues such as climate change, loss of biodiversity, and environmental degradation, like a wildfire sweepin' through the land, require collective and long-term solutions, like a united team of cowboys workin' together to contain the blaze.

The urgency of addressing these global challenges, like a call for quick action on the trail, cannot be overstated. It's crucial for nations to come together, like a caravan cooperatin' to navigate rough terrain, and prioritize the well-being of the planet and future generations over immediate gains.

Fostering international cooperation, like skilled wranglers supportin' each other on the frontier, and promoting sustainable practices, like a careful trail guide considerin' the environment, can help address pressing global issues and protect the planet for generations to come.

While it can be challenging to find common ground, like a difficult river crossin' on the trail, the shared responsibility to protect the planet calls for collective action, like a determined team of cowboys steerin' toward a common destination.

As citizens, like vigilant wranglers watchin' over the herd, we can play a role in advocatin' for responsible environmental policies and supportin' leaders who prioritize the health of the planet, like a supportive partner on the journey to a more sustainable future.

Me

Well now, enlightened preference voting sounds like a trail worth explorin'. It's a notion where folks cast their votes with a clearer view, like a cowboy eyein' the whole range before decidin' which way to ride. Reckon it might just be a superior route compared to our current system. What's got you leanin' toward this enlightened preference, and do you see it as a sunrise on the political horizon?

Sage Cowboy

Enlightened preference voting, also known as ranked-choice voting or instant-runoff voting, is indeed an alternative voting system that has been proposed as a potential improvement over some aspects of the current electoral systems, like a different trail to reach the destination.

In enlightened preference voting, voters rank candidates in order of preference, like a group of cowboys votin' for their preferred trail guide. If no candidate receives a majority of first-preference votes, like a clear path on the trail, the candidate with the fewest first-preference votes is eliminated, and their votes are transferred to the voters' next preferred candidate, like explorin' other paths on the trail.

This process continues until a candidate achieves a majority of votes, like a chosen trail guide gainin' the support of the majority of the caravan.

Enlightened preference voting can have several potential benefits, like a smoother journey on the trail:

Reducing Strategic Voting: Voters can rank candidates based on their true preferences, like an honest cowboy sharin' their thoughts, without fear of "wasting" their vote or voting strategically.

Encouraging More Diverse Candidates: The system can allow for a broader range of candidates to participate in elections, like a diverse group of cowboys joinin' the trail.

Building Consensus: The winning candidate is more likely to have broader support from the electorate, like a united team of cowboys workin' together on the frontier.

However, like any electoral system, enlightened preference voting is not without its challenges and critics, like various terrains on the trail. Implementing such a system may require changes to existing electoral laws and systems, like adjustin' the gear for a new trail.

Additionally, public education on how the system works, like explainin' the map for a new trail, is crucial to ensure voters understand the process and have confidence in the electoral system.

Different countries and jurisdictions have different electoral systems, like cowboys adaptin' to different trails. Decisions about voting systems involve considerations of historical, cultural, and political contexts, like choosin' the best route for the caravan.

Ultimately, the quest for an ideal voting system, like findin' the right path on the trail, involves careful assessment and deliberation, like thoughtful cowboys plannin' their journey together.

Me

You're wranglin' with a valid point there, partner. Even with enlightened preference voting, if the corral is filled with lackluster candidates, it's like tryin' to rope a tumbleweed – not much to grab onto. The strength of the candidates is the backbone of any political roundup. What changes do you reckon might bring forth a herd of stronger contenders in the political show?

Sage Cowboy

You raise a valid point, partner. Enlightened preference voting, while offering potential benefits, like a different approach to the trail, may not directly address the issue of weak candidates participatin' in the electoral process.

The presence of weak candidates can be influenced by various factors, like different elements affectin' the caravan's composition. Some of these factors include the availability of financial resources, party support, media coverage, and public perceptions, like factors shapin' the reputation of cowboys on the trail.

To ensure a robust and competitive electoral landscape, like a diverse group of skilled cowboys joinin' the trail, there might be a need for additional measures and reforms, like takin' steps to attract the best riders.

Encourage Participation: Policies that encourage diverse candidates to participate, like offerin' incentives to experienced cowboys, can help increase the pool of qualified contenders.

Campaign Finance Reform: Implementin' campaign finance regulations, like settin' fair rules on the trail, can reduce the influence of money in politics and level the playin' field.

Access to Media: Ensuring fair and equitable access to media coverage, like providin' equal opportunities to all riders, can help promote the visibility of candidates with different backgrounds and ideas.

Transparent Candidate Selection: Political parties can play a role in selectin' strong candidates, like a team of cowboys choosin' the best riders, by adoptin' transparent and inclusive candidate selection processes.

Civic Education: Enhancin' civic education and voter engagement, like equippin' all members of the caravan with knowledge, can help voters make informed choices.

While enlightened preference voting may not directly address the issue of weak candidates, like addressin' a specific challenge on the trail, it can contribute to a more representative and responsive electoral system.

As with any electoral reform, like plannin' a new trail route, a comprehensive approach that considers various factors and engages all stakeholders is essential in creatin' a more vibrant and effective democratic process.

Me

Well, reckon that's an astute observation, partner. If the notion of Mediacare is about ensurin' every citizen has a fair shot at the campfire of information, then it's like providin' a level playin' field for all. What's your vision for this Mediacare, and how do you see it roundin' up access to information for folks on every corner of the prairie?

Sage Cowboy

Apologies for any misunderstanding, partner. I can see how the suggestion in point number 3 aligns with your idea of "Mediacare" to ensure universal access to media.

If "Mediacare" refers to a system that provides all citizens with access to diverse and unbiased media sources, like a provision of essential resources on the trail, then it could indeed contribute to a more informed and engaged electorate, like equippin' all members of the caravan with the right tools.

Having access to reliable and diverse media outlets, like havin' access to different perspectives on the trail, can empower citizens to make well-informed decisions and participate more effectively in the democratic process, like bein' equipped to navigate challenging terrain.

Ensuring equitable media access, like ensurin' all cowboys have access to the same resources, can promote democratic values and facilitate open and constructive dialogue, like fosterin' good communication on the trail.

As with any proposal or policy, like considerin' a new route on the trail, it's essential to carefully assess the feasibility, impact, and implementation of such an idea. Public discussion and deliberation, like engagin' in open conversations among cowboys, can be valuable in shaping and refining initiatives to strengthen democracy and media access.

If you have more details or specific ideas about "Mediacare" or any other topic you'd like to explore further, feel free to share, and we can continue our journey together!

Me

Now, that's a notion that's got some spurs to it, partner. Sponsoring social media ahead of the election is like throwin' open the saloon doors for a lively town hall meetin'. And if candidates ain't tendin' to the concerns of the folks, reckon they oughta be showin' the exit by the electoral wranglers. How do you see this idea ropin' in a more engaged and accountable political showdown?

Sage Cowboy

Your proposal suggests a way to enhance access to information and promote dialogue between voters and candidates during election periods, like settin' up rest stops along the trail for discussions.

Sponsoring social media platforms to provide live platforms for each constituency, like creatin' information hubs on the trail, can be an innovative approach to ensure widespread access to political debates and discussions, like providin' a platform for cowboys to share their thoughts.

By offering equal opportunities for candidates to engage with voters and present their ideas, like creatin' fair conditions on the trail, such initiatives can contribute to a more informed electorate, like well-prepared cowboys ready for the journey.

Additionally, holdin' candidates accountable for fulfillin' the interests of voters, like a quality assurance for riders, can strengthen the democratic process, like maintainin' the integrity of the caravan.

However, as with any electoral reform or policy, like plannin' the route for the caravan, there are various factors to consider:

Ensuring Fairness: Measures should be in place to ensure fair and impartial access to social media platforms, like makin' sure all cowboys have equal chances.

Balancing Regulations: Striking a balance between accountability and the freedom of candidates to express their views, like findin' the right pace on the trail, is important.

Avoiding Biases: Electoral authorities must remain unbiased, like an impartial trail guide, in evaluating candidates' performances and interests.

Public Awareness: Public education and awareness campaigns, like knowin' the map for the trail, can help citizens understand the importance of their role in the electoral process.

Incorporatin' public opinion and engagin' in open dialogue, like communicatin' among cowboys on the trail, can help refine and improve such proposals to strengthen democracy and voter engagement.

If you have any more ideas to discuss or other topics to explore, feel free to share, and we can continue our journey together!

Me

Much obliged, partner. It seems like in the current scenario, the political trail is mighty foggy. Voters castin' their ballots without a clear view of the candidates is akin to ridin' blindfolded into a dust storm. Engagin' with voters and liftin' the veil on the candidates could be the sunshine needed to clear the haze. The notion of tribal and religious loyalty swayin' votes is a challenge indeed. How do you reckon we could break through this fog and bring in a breeze of informed and independent choices?

Sage Cowboy

You've highlighted some significant challenges in the current electoral landscape, partner. The issues you mentioned, like obstacles on the trail, can indeed impact the democratic process and citizen engagement.

Lack of Information: The lack of information about candidates can lead to uninformed voting decisions, like blindfolded cowboys navigatin' the trail. Voters may not have access to comprehensive information about candidates' backgrounds, qualifications, and policy positions.

Candidate Engagement: Some candidates may not prioritize engaging directly with voters, like cowboys avoidin' conversation with the rest of the caravan. This lack of interaction can hinder meaningful dialogue and limit the opportunity for voters to assess the candidates' suitability for office.

Tribal and Religious Influences: In some multicultural communities, like different groups of cowboys followin' their own leaders, tribal or religious affiliations can play a significant role in influencing voting behavior. This can lead to bloc voting based on identity rather than a thorough evaluation of candidates' platforms.

Addressin' these challenges may require a multi-faceted approach, like a coordinated strategy for traversin' difficult terrain:

Voter Education: Initiatives to promote voter education, like holdin' workshops to learn about the trail ahead, can help empower citizens with knowledge about the electoral process and candidates.

Candidate Outreach: Encouragin' candidates to actively engage with voters, like approachable cowboys communicatin' with others, can foster greater transparency and accountability.

Independent Media: Supportin' independent and diverse media sources, like varied perspectives on the trail, can provide voters with balanced and unbiased information about candidates.

Civic Organizations: Engagin' civic organizations, like gatherin' cowboys for constructive discussions, can help facilitate community dialogues and encourage informed voting decisions.

Transparency and Accountability: Advocatin' for measures that promote transparency and accountability in the electoral process, like clear rules on the trail, can help build trust and confidence in the system.

Encouragin' Inclusivity: Efforts to promote inclusivity and representation, like welcomin' all cowboys to participate, can contribute to a more diverse and engaged electorate.

Improvin' the democratic process requires collective effort, like a united team of cowboys collaboratin' on the frontier. By addressin' these challenges, we can work towards a more vibrant and participatory democracy, like a smooth ride for the entire caravan.

If you have more ideas to discuss or need further insights on any topic, feel free to share, and we can continue our journey together!

Me

That's a sage piece of advice, partner. Encouragin' voters to mosey on down the trail of information, checkin' a candidate's knowledge, attitude, past deeds, and plans for the community is like givin' them a map to navigate the political terrain. Lookin' beyond the brand of a national or state-level party and sizin' up the local representative is akin to checkin' the horse's hooves before hittin' the trail. How do you reckon we can spread this approach far and wide, so every voter can saddle up with an informed choice?

Sage Cowboy

You've provided excellent advice, partner! Your suggestions highlight the importance of informed and thoughtful voting, like a well-prepared cowboy surveyin' the trail ahead, to ensure that candidates truly represent the interests and values of the community.

Engagin' in the following steps, like takin' care of the horses before the journey:

Gather Information: Seekin' information about candidates' knowledge, attitudes, and past experiences, like gatherin' information about the trail conditions, can help voters make informed decisions.

Assess Plans and Policies: Understandin' candidates' plans for the betterment of the community, like examinin' a trail guide's route plan, can provide insight into their vision and priorities.

Consider Local Representation: Evaluatin' candidates based on their suitability for local representation, like considerin' a cowboy's ability to navigate specific terrain, is crucial, regardless of their national or state-level party affiliation.

Look Beyond Partisanship: Movin' beyond blind loyalty to a political party, like widenin' the perspective on the trail, allows voters to focus on the individual candidate's merits and qualifications.

By takin' these steps, like a vigilant cowboy scoutin' the best route, voters can make choices that align with their community's needs and interests. A well-informed electorate, like a well-prepared caravan, is essential for a robust and responsive democratic process.

Encouragin' civic engagement, like a supportive team of cowboys, and promoting the importance of informed voting, like communicatin' about the journey ahead, can strengthen democracy and contribute to effective local representation.

If you have any more insights to share or further ideas to discuss, feel free to let me know, and we can continue our journey together!

Me

Sacha Baron Cohen, in his unique way, used humor and satire to highlight certain aspects of American democracy. His opening question, "Why are you guys so anti-dictators?" is a satirical way of drawing attention to the contradictions or challenges within the democratic system. He often employs such comedic tactics to provoke thought and reflection on societal issues. What are your thoughts on Cohen's approach to addressing democratic themes through humor?

Sage Cowboy

I am familiar with Sacha Baron Cohen, a well-known British actor, comedian, and satirist known for his unique and often controversial style of humor. He is famous for his various comedic characters, including Ali G, Borat Sagdiyev, and Brüno Gehard.

Sacha Baron Cohen is known for using satire and parody to shed light on social and political issues, often employing his characters to expose hypocrisy and absurdities in society.

While I don't have access to all information, I can understand that Sacha Baron Cohen's speech mocking American democracy could be in line with his satirical style, like a humorous skit on the trail. It's not uncommon for comedians to use humor to highlight flaws and challenges within political systems, like revealin' hidden obstacles on the trail.

Satire has a long history of being used to critique and question those in power, like a cowboy jestin' with his fellow riders. It can serve as a way to provoke thought and encourage audiences to reflect on the state of their democracy, like promptin' cowboys to consider the journey ahead.

If you have specific details about the speech or would like to discuss the topic further, feel free to share, and we can explore it together!

Me

The short-sightedness of today's democratic wranglin' is as clear as a desert sunrise.

Sage Cowboy

You've pointed out a common concern, partner. The short-sightedness or myopia in modern democratic politics can indeed be evident in various aspects of the political landscape, like a limited view of the trail ahead.

Here are a few examples of how myopia can manifest in democratic politics:

Short-Term Focus: Politicians may prioritize immediate gains and short-term goals, like lookin' only at the next few miles of the trail, instead of addressing long-term challenges and solutions.

Populist Policies: Some politicians may adopt populist policies to gain popularity in the short term, like a quick gallop to win applause, without considering the broader and sustainable implications.

Partisan Polarization: The focus on party politics and partisan interests, like divisiveness among cowboys on the trail, can hinder cooperation and compromise for the greater good.

Media Cycle Influence: The 24/7 news cycle and social media-driven politics, like swift gusts of information, can encourage reactive and sensationalized decision-making.

Neglecting Future Generations: Policymakers may neglect the needs and concerns of future generations, like ignorin' potential challenges and opportunities down the trail.

Lack of Comprehensive Solutions: Some issues require complex and long-term solutions, like careful trail plannin', but may be addressed with band-aid fixes that don't tackle the root causes.

Addressin' myopia in democratic politics requires a shift in approach, like a change in the way cowboys navigate the trail:

Long-Term Vision: Encouragin' politicians to have a broader and more long-term vision, like settin' sights on the destination, can lead to more sustainable and impactful policies.

Fact-Based Decision-Making: Promotin' evidence-based policymaking, like relyin' on reliable trail information, can help move beyond reactive politics and focus on effective solutions.

Inclusivity and Cooperation: Fosterin' collaboration and inclusivity among political parties, like a united caravan, can lead to more comprehensive and durable policies.

Civic Engagement: Encouragin' active citizen engagement, like communicatin' among cowboys, can help hold politicians accountable for their actions and decisions.

Education and Awareness: Raisin' awareness about the importance of long-term planning and the consequences of short-sighted policies, like explainin' the map ahead, can help shape public discourse.

Ultimately, like traversin' the trail with care, it's essential for citizens, policymakers, and all members of the democratic process to work together to address the challenges of myopia and create a more sustainable and responsible political environment.

Me

Seems like voters are searchin' for swift solutions and instant remedies.

Sage Cowboy

You're absolutely right, partner. Just like politicians, voters can also seek quick fixes or immediate solutions to complex issues, like a desire for a rapid solution on the trail.

Voters may be drawn to promises or policies that offer simple and straightforward answers to complicated problems, like a shortcut to reach the destination. Some factors that contribute to this preference for quick fixes include:

Information Overload: In today's fast-paced world, like a whirlwind on the trail, voters are often inundated with information from various sources. This can lead to a desire for easy and digestible solutions.

Sound Bites and Media Messaging: Political campaigns and media coverage, like brief calls from one cowboy to another, may prioritize catchy sound bites and slogans, which can oversimplify complex issues.

Lack of Time: Many voters, like busy cowboys on the trail, may not have the luxury of dedicating extensive time to researching and understanding in-depth policy proposals.

Emotional Appeal: Some candidates or policies may appeal to voters' emotions, like a heartwarming tale by the campfire, rather than presenting detailed plans and evidence-based approaches.

However, like thoughtful cowboys plannin' their journey, it's essential for voters to take a more comprehensive and informed approach:

Educate Yourself: Take the time to research and understand candidates' positions, like studyin' the trail map, and the potential implications of their policies.

Look Beyond Sound Bites: Seek out in-depth information and analysis, like explorin' different aspects of the trail, to gain a deeper understanding of the issues.

Consider Long-Term Impact: Evaluate policies based on their potential long-term consequences, like considerin' the journey ahead, rather than just short-term benefits.

Hold Candidates Accountable: Assess candidates based on their track record, like a cowboy's experience on the trail, and their ability to deliver on their promises.

Engage in Discourse: Discuss and debate with fellow voters, like communicatin' with other cowboys, to gain different perspectives and insights.

By adoptin' a more thoughtful and engaged approach, like a united team of cowboys plannin' their route, voters can play a crucial role in promotin' responsible and effective governance. It's the collective responsibility of citizens and policymakers to prioritize the long-term well-being of the community, like keepin' the caravan steady on the trail, over quick fixes.

Me

Folks might be chasin' quick fixes because the cost of livin' is climbin' like a stubborn mountain, and snaggin' a homestead is near impossible.

Sage Cowboy

You've hit the nail on the head, partner. The rising cost of living and the increasing unaffordability of housing can undoubtedly contribute to voters' desire for quick fixes and immediate solutions, like urgent attempts to find shelter on the trail.

The challenges posed by the cost of living and housing affordability can have significant impacts on individuals and families, like experiencing rough terrain on the trail. Some key factors that contribute to these issues include:

Inflation and Economic Pressures: Increasing costs of essential goods and services, like the rising cost of supplies on the trail, can strain household budgets and make it harder to make ends meet.

Housing Market Dynamics: Factors such as limited housing supply, like scarce resting places on the trail, and high demand can drive up property prices and rental costs.

Wage Stagnation: The slow growth of wages compared to the cost of living, like a lagging pace on the trail, can exacerbate financial struggles for many individuals and families.

Financial Inequality: Economic disparities, like differences in resources among cowboys on the trail, can lead to unequal access to affordable housing and basic necessities.

These economic challenges can understandably fuel a sense of urgency among voters, like the need to find quick solutions for their immediate needs.

To address these issues effectively, like findin' the right trail route, policymakers must consider both short-term relief measures and long-term systemic changes:

Short-Term Relief: Implementing short-term measures, like providin' temporary rest stops on the trail, such as targeted financial assistance or housing support, can alleviate immediate hardships.

Affordable Housing Initiatives: Investing in affordable housing programs, like buildin' more accessible lodging along the trail, can create long-term solutions to address housing affordability.

Economic Growth and Job Opportunities: Policies that promote economic growth and job creation, like clearin' the trail for smoother travel, can lead to higher wages and improved financial stability.

Social Safety Nets: Strengthenin' social safety net programs, like providin' essential resources on the trail, can offer support to those facing financial hardships.

Inclusive Economic Policies: Ensuring economic policies that benefit all segments of society, like a fair distribution of resources on the trail, can contribute to reducing economic inequality.

By balancin' short-term relief with long-term systemic changes, like a well-thought-out trail plan, policymakers can work towards addressing the root causes of economic challenges and providing more stable and sustainable solutions for voters.

Me

Some reckon it might just be a capitalist plot, keepin' voters roped in by the relentless struggle of financial woes.

Sage Cowboy

The notion of a conspiracy to keep voters overwhelmed by financial hardship is a complex and debated topic, partner. While some individuals and groups may argue that certain economic and political systems perpetuate or exacerbate financial hardships for the majority, others may see these issues as the result of complex societal and global factors, like navigatin' challenging terrain on the trail.

It's important to recognize that economic systems, like the trail route, can be influenced by various actors, including policymakers, businesses, and other stakeholders. Some factors that can contribute to financial hardships and inequalities include:

Economic Policies: The design and implementation of economic policies, like plannin' the trail, can have a significant impact on wealth distribution, job opportunities, and housing affordability.

Global Economic Trends: Factors in the global economy, like external factors affectin' the trail conditions, can influence national economies and impact living costs.

Technological Changes: Advancements in technology, like new tools for the trail, can affect job markets and create shifts in industries, leading to challenges for some workers.

Market Concentration: In certain sectors, like havin' a narrow path on the trail, market concentration and lack of competition can result in higher prices and limited options for consumers.

Regulatory Environment: The regulatory framework, like settin' rules for travelin' on the trail, can influence business practices and income inequality.

While some critics may argue that certain economic and political interests perpetuate financial hardships for their benefit, others may view these challenges as unintended consequences of complex systems, like the unpredictable nature of the trail.

Addressin' financial hardships requires a comprehensive approach, like plannin' for the diverse terrain ahead:

Inclusive Economic Policies: Adoptin' economic policies that prioritize inclusive growth, like considerin' the needs of all cowboys on the trail, can help reduce financial disparities.

Social Safety Nets: Strengthenin' social safety nets, like providin' essential resources on the trail, can provide support to those facing economic difficulties.

Affordable Housing Initiatives: Investin' in affordable housing programs, like creatin' more accessible resting places on the trail, can improve housing affordability.

Job Training and Education: Offerin' job training and educational opportunities, like providin' useful skills for the trail, can enhance employability and income potential.

Civic Engagement: Engagin' citizens in the democratic process, like holdin' open discussions among cowboys, can empower them to advocate for their interests and influence policy decisions.

Ultimately, like a united caravan confrontin' challenges, collaboratin' and workin' towards solutions that benefit all members of society is essential in addressing financial hardships and building a more equitable and sustainable future.

Me

It's plain as day: the interests of voters and capitalists are driftin' apart like two ornery cowboys headin' in opposite directions.

Sage Cowboy

You've made a keen observation, partner. It is true that the interests of voters and capitalists can often appear to be at odds, like two cowboys headin' in different directions on the trail.

The interests of voters, like the caravan's destination, are typically focused on:

Economic Security: Voters often prioritize policies that promote job stability, fair wages, and access to affordable housing and healthcare.

Social Safety Nets: Many voters advocate for robust social safety net programs that provide support during times of financial hardship or personal challenges.

Education and Opportunity: Voters often seek policies that invest in education and skill development, like preparin' for the journey ahead, to create better opportunities for themselves and their families.

Environmental Sustainability: Concern for the environment, like preservin' the natural beauty of the trail, is often an important issue for voters who seek policies to address climate change and promote sustainable practices.

On the other hand, the interests of capitalists, like the pursuit of individual goals, are often centered on:

Profit Maximisation: Capitalists typically prioritize policies that maximize profits and promote business growth, like seekin' rewards along the trail.

Regulatory Flexibility: Some capitalists advocate for policies that provide flexibility in regulations, like findin' alternative paths on the trail, to promote business innovation and expansion.

Taxation and Regulation: Capitalists may push for tax policies and regulations that they believe support investment and entrepreneurship, like makin' financial decisions on the trail.

Market Liberalisation: Many capitalists favour policies that promote free markets and reduce government intervention, like movin' freely on the trail.

While these interests can sometimes diverge, it's important to recognize that the relationship between voters and capitalists is complex, like the varied interactions among cowboys on the trail. There are instances where their interests align, such as in the creation of jobs and economic growth, which can benefit both groups.

Addressin' the tensions between the interests of voters and capitalists may require thoughtful and balanced policymakin', like negotiatin' the trail route:

Inclusive Economic Policies: Policymakers can strive to create economic policies that consider the needs of both voters and businesses, like findin' common ground on the trail.

Public-Private Collaboration: Encouragin' collaboration between the public and private sectors, like cowboys workin' together, can lead to solutions that benefit both groups.

Transparency and Accountability: Promotin' transparency and accountability in policymakin', like clear communication on the trail, can build trust between voters and capitalists.

Advocacy and Engagement: Encouragin' citizens and businesses to engage in the democratic process, like active participation on the trail, can help shape policies that reflect a wide range of interests.

Balancin' the interests of voters and capitalists, like maintainin' harmony among cowboys on the trail, is an ongoing challenge in democratic societies. By workin' together and seekin' common ground, we can strive to create a more inclusive and equitable future for all.

Me

Seems like the capitalists are set on exploitin' the public, the very voters. Without that exploitation and coin clinkin', capitalism might crumble like a shaky Ponzi scheme.

Sage Cowboy

The relationship between capitalism and the public, including voters, is a complex and multifaceted one, partner. While some critics argue that capitalism inherently leads to the exploitation of the public, others believe that it can foster economic growth and innovation that benefits society as a whole, like a dynamic trail with various twists and turns.

Key aspects to consider in the relationship between capitalism and the public include:

Profit Motive: Capitalism's fundamental principle is the pursuit of profit, like a primary goal for cowboys to reach their destination. Some argue that this focus on profit can lead to the exploitation of workers and consumers if left unchecked.

Wealth Inequality: Critics of capitalism point out that it can lead to significant wealth disparities, like gaps between cowboys in the caravan, with some individuals and corporations amassing vast amounts of wealth while others struggle to make ends meet.

Market Regulation: Advocates of capitalism often emphasize the importance of minimal government intervention, like leavin' cowboys to navigate the trail independently, to allow markets to function efficiently. However, critics argue that lack of regulation can lead to abuses and exploitation.

Corporate Social Responsibility: Some companies embrace the concept of corporate social responsibility, like a commitment to the well-being of the caravan, by considering social and environmental impacts alongside profits.

Consumer Choice: Capitalism can provide consumers with a wide range of choices, like various paths on the trail, in products and services, giving them the freedom to make decisions based on their preferences and needs.

To address concerns about exploitation and wealth inequality, policymakers, like trail guides, may implement measures to:

Ensure Labour Protections: Implement and enforce labour laws and regulations to protect workers' rights, like safeguardin' cowboys' well-being on the trail.

Promote Fair Competition: Encourage competition in the market, like a level playing field on the trail, to prevent monopolies and foster innovation.

Progressive Taxation: Consider progressive taxation, like a fair distribution of resources on the trail, to address wealth disparities and fund social programs.

Consumer Protection: Strengthen consumer protection laws, like safeguardin' cowboys from predatory practices, to ensure fair treatment and safety.

Support Small Businesses: Foster an environment that supports small businesses, like providin' a space for small caravans on the trail, to promote economic diversity.

Balancing the interests of capitalism and the well-being of the public, like coordinatin' a harmonious journey, is an ongoing challenge that requires thoughtful policymaking and public engagement.

As we continue on this trail of discussion, feel free to share any further insights or questions, and we'll continue to explore together!

Me

The steps these policymakers take feel like dribblin' a few drops of water in the parched mouth of a cowboy stranded in the scorchin' desert. I reckon, policymakers ought to wrangle more by saddlin' capitalists with taxes and givin' folks free rides on public transport, free access to the media corral, and free lessons on the economics and ways of managin' the financial herd.

Sage Cowboy

Your perspective highlights the importance of comprehensive and impactful policy measures, partner. Indeed, droppin' a few drops of water may not be enough to quench the thirst of a cowboy lost in the desert, and policymakers should consider more substantial actions to address the challenges faced by the public.

Your suggestions of taxing capitalists and using the revenue to provide free public transport, free access to media, and financial education are all potential measures that could have a significant impact on society, like providin' essential resources to those in need on the trail.

Here's a closer look at how these measures could benefit the public:

Taxing Capitalists: Implementin' progressive taxation on high-income earners and corporations could generate additional revenue for public services and social programs. This could help bridge the gap between wealthier individuals and those with fewer resources, like ensurin' a fair distribution of resources on the trail.

Free Public Transport: Providin' free or subsidized public transport can improve accessibility and mobility for all members of society, like offerin' a convenient and affordable path for cowboys to reach their destinations. This can particularly benefit low-income individuals and reduce the burden of transportation costs on households.

Free Access to Media: Ensuring free access to unbiased and reliable media can promote transparency and democracy, like sharin' vital information with all cowboys on the trail. It can empower citizens to make informed decisions and engage in public discourse.

Financial Education: Offerin' free financial education can empower individuals with the knowledge and skills to manage their finances better, like equippin' cowboys with essential navigation skills for the journey. This can help promote financial stability and improve overall economic well-being.

Implementin' these measures would require careful consideration and collaboration among policymakers, the private sector, and the public, like a coordinated effort on the trail. Balancin' the interests of different stakeholders and evaluatin' the potential impact of these policies would be crucial to ensure their effectiveness.

It's important to remember that policy changes and societal improvements often require incremental progress, like steady steps taken on the trail. While a complete transformation may not happen overnight, consistent efforts toward more equitable policies can make a meaningful difference in the lives of individuals and communities.

As we continue to discuss, let's keep explorin' various ideas and solutions, like a team of cowboys collaboratin' to navigate the trail together!

Me

Well, partner, reckon it's time to rustle up a roundup of our talkin'. How 'bout you wrangle up a one-page summary of all them recommendations you've been mullin' over in this discourse? Let's corral them thoughts and see what's been brewin' on this trail we've been ridin'. Yeehaw!

Sage Cowboy

Well, partner, here's a roundup of the wisdom we've wrangled in our talk about how capitalism, democracy, and the folks' interests dance together on this dusty trail. Yeehaw!

Title: Navigating the Trail of Capitalism and Democracy

In our discussion, we explored the intricate relationship between capitalism, democracy, and the interests of the public, drawing parallels with a caravan navigating a challenging trail. Here are some key takeaways:

1. Complex Interplay: The relationship between capitalism and democracy is intricate. While capitalism can foster

innovation and economic growth, it also raises concerns about wealth inequality and exploitation.

2. Democracy as a Tool: Democracy, when functioning effectively, acts as a tool for citizens to voice their concerns and shape policies. However, the influence of money in politics and the two-party dominance pose challenges.

3. Exploitation Concerns: There's a concern that capitalism, driven by a profit motive, may exploit the public. Striking a balance between business interests and the well-being of citizens is crucial.

4. Public Engagement: Encouraging citizens to actively engage in the democratic process is essential. Informed voting, advocacy, and holding policymakers accountable contribute to a healthier democracy.

5. Policy Measures: Policymakers play a vital role. Measures such as progressive taxation, support for small businesses, and consumer protection can help address wealth disparities and promote fairness.

6. Comprehensive Solutions: Dropping a few drops of water in the desert isn't enough. Policymakers should consider more substantial measures, like taxing capitalists to fund free public transport, media access, and financial education.

7. Incremental Progress: Transformation takes time. Incremental progress, consistent efforts, and a balance between various

interests are essential for creating a more equitable and sustainable future.

In navigating the trail of capitalism and democracy, the key lies in fostering collaboration, transparency, and policies that prioritize the well-being of the entire caravan. The journey may be challenging, but with thoughtful navigation, the caravan can reach a destination where the interests of all are considered and respected.

Me

Much obliged, partner, for sharin' this campfire conversation.

Sage Cowboy

You're very welcome! If you ever decide to hit the trail of conversation again or have more questions in the future, feel free to saddle up and drop by. Happy trails, partner!

Me

Happy trails Sage Cowboy!

Sage Cowboy

Happy trails to you too! Take care, and may your journey be filled with clear skies and open trails. If you ever need a chat, the campfire is always burning. Adiós, partner!

Me

Adiós Master!

****

www.ingramcontent.com/pod-product-compliance
Lightning Source LLC
Chambersburg PA
CBHW070804260726

48660CB00005B/1700

www.ingramcontent.com/pod-product-compliance
Lightning Source LLC
Chambersburg PA
CBHW070804260726

48660CB00005B/1700